TAKE
NOTE!

TO ACCOMPANY

PSYCHOLOGY
Mind, Brain, and Culture

Second Edition

Drew Westen
Harvard University

JOHN WILEY & SONS, INC.
New York • Chichester • Weinheim
Brisbane • Singapore • Toronto

BN 0-471-32200-8

ed in the United States of America

8 7 6 5 4

ed and bound by Courier Westford, Inc.

TABLE OF CONTENTS

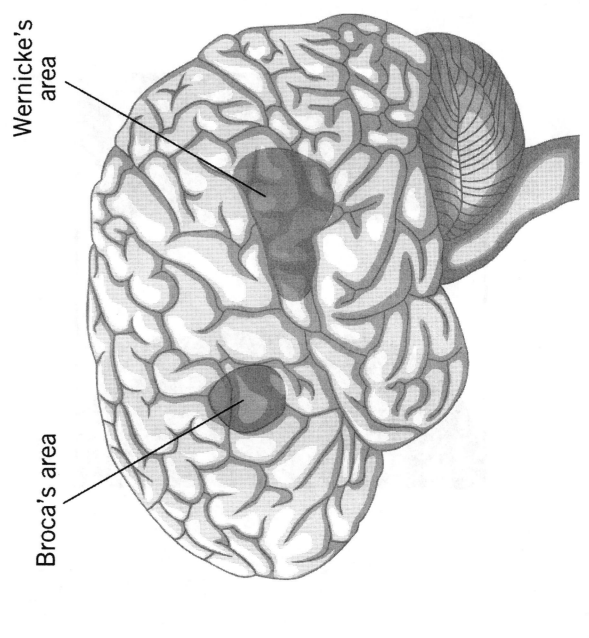

Wernicke's area

Broca's area

Westen, 2e Fig. 1.1

1

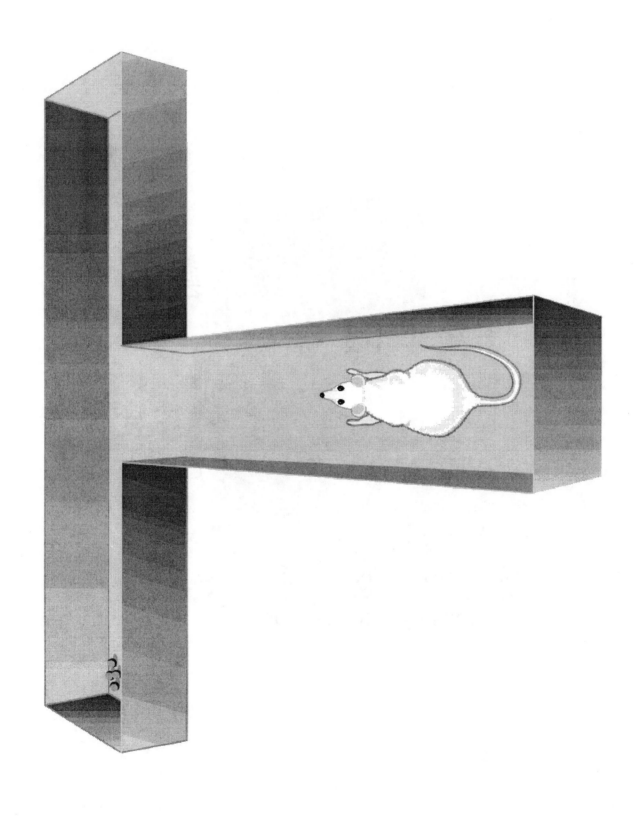

Westen, 2e Fig. 1.3

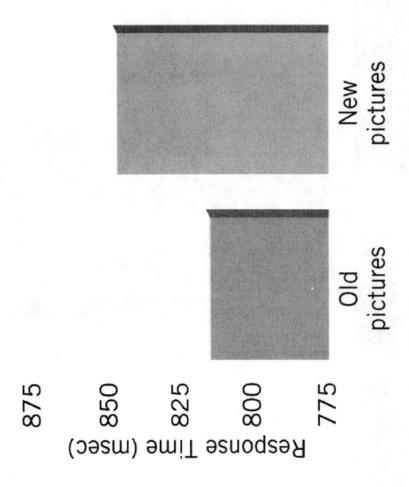

4

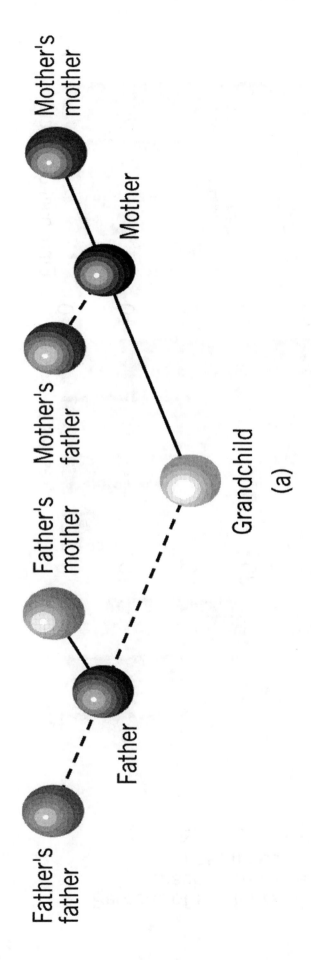

Father's
father

Father's
mother

Mother's
father

Mother's
mother

Father

Mother

Grandchild

(a)

Westen, 2e Fig. 1.7a

© 1999 John Wiley and Sons, Inc.

5

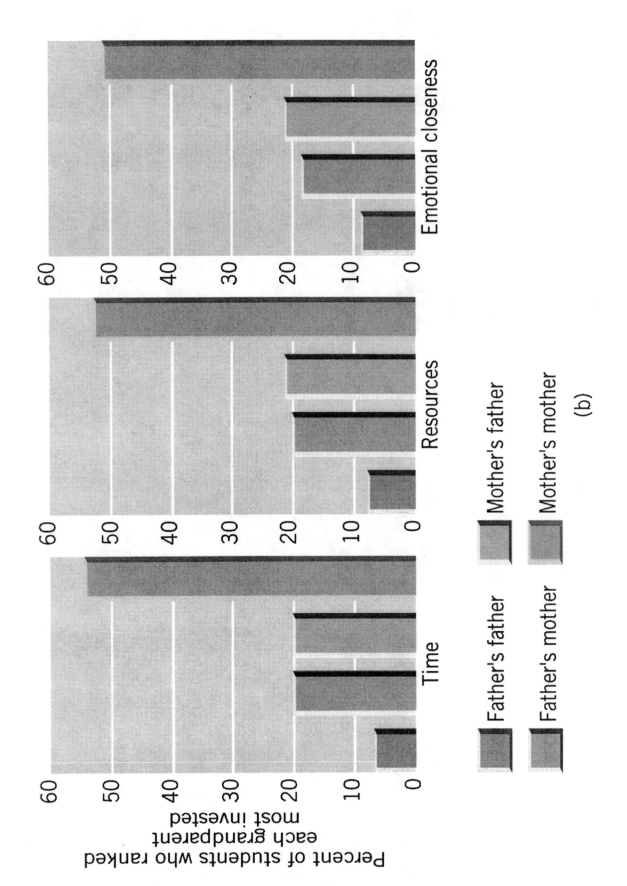

Westen, 2e Fig. 1.7b

(b)

Father's father

Father's mother

Mother's father

Mother's mother

Emotional closeness

Resources

Time

Percent of students who ranked
each grandparent
most invested

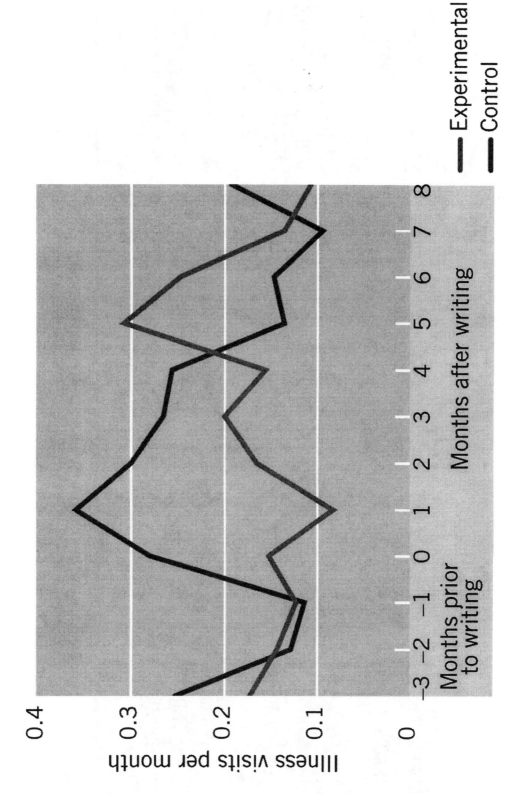

(Figure adapted from Pennebaker et al., 1990, p. 533)

Westen, 2e Fig. 2.1

© 1999 John Wiley and Sons, Inc.

A THEORETICAL FRAMEWORK	A STANDARDIZED PROCEDURE	GENERALIZABILITY	OBJECTIVE MEASUREMENT
Systematic way of organizing and explaining observations	Procedure that is the same for all subjects except where variation is introduced to test a hypothesis	Sample that is representative of the population	Measures that are reliable (that produce consistent results)
Hypothesis that flows from the theory or from an important question		Procedure that is sensible and relevant to circumstances outside the laboratory	Measures that are valid (that assess the dimensions they purport to assess)

Westen, 2e Fig. 2.2

OPERATIONALIZING VARIABLES

Converting abstract concepts into testable form

DEVELOPING A STANDARDIZED PROCEDURE

Setting up experimental conditions and control; attending to demand characteristics (subjects' perceptions of the researcher's goals that could influence their responses); attending to researcher bias

SELECTING AND ASSIGNING SUBJECTS

Randomly assigning subjects to different conditions

APPLYING STATISTICAL TECHNIQUES

Describing the data and determining the likelihood that differences between the conditions reflect causality or chance

FRAMING A HYPOTHESIS

Predicting the relations among two or more variables

DRAWING CONCLUSIONS

Evaluating whether or not the data support the hypothesis; suggesting future studies to address limitations and new questions raised by the study

Westen, 2e Fig. 2.4

© 1999 John Wiley and Sons, Inc.

9

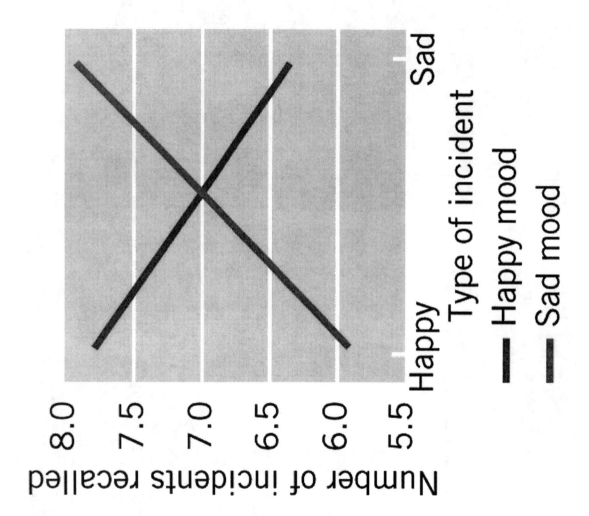

(Figure adapted from Bower, 1991)

Westen, 2e Fig. 2.5

© 1999 John Wiley and Sons, Inc.

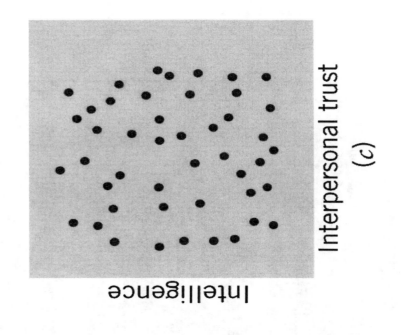

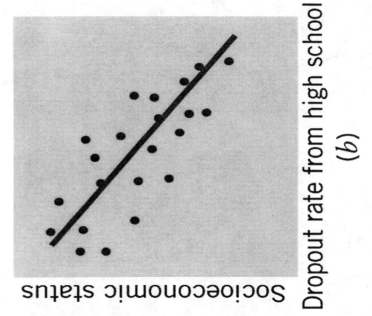

Weight

Height

(a)

Socioeconomic status

Dropout rate from high school

(b)

Intelligence

Interpersonal trust

(c)

© 1999 John Wiley and Sons, Inc.

Westen, 2e Fig. 2.6

11

1. Assess the study's theoretical framework.

Does the theory make sense?
Does the hypothesis make sense?
Are terms defined logically and consistently?

2. Assess the adequacy and appropriateness of the sample.

Is it representative of the population of interest?
Is it of sufficient size to test the hypothesis?

3. Assess the adequacy of the measures and procedures.

Are the measures reliable and valid?
Did the investigators properly control confounding variables?

4. Examine the data.

Do the data demonstrate what the authors claim?
Could the data be explained some other way?

5. Examine the conclusions drawn by the investigators.

Do the conclusions follow from the data?
Does the study have limitations that affect the interpretation or generalizability of the findings?
Can the findings be understood in the context of previous research?

6. Consider the meaningfulness of the study.

Does the study pass the "so what" test?
Do the theory and data shed any new light on the phenomenon under investigation?

7. Evaluate the ethics of the study.

Did the costs outweigh the benefits?
Did the investigators carefully consider the welfare of human and animal subjects?

Westen, 2e Fig. 2.8

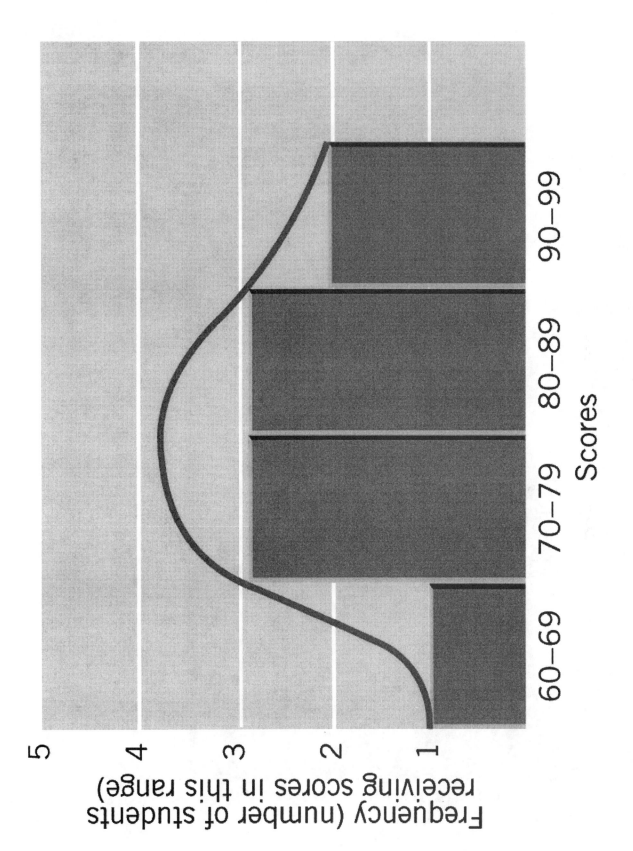

Scores

Frequency (number of students receiving scores in this range)

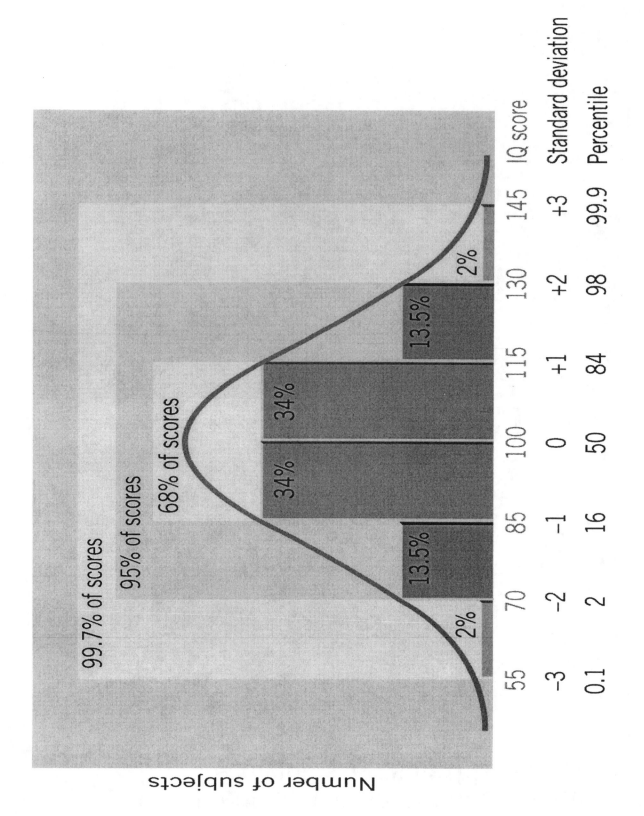

© 1999 John Wiley and Sons, Inc.

Westen, 2e Fig. 2S.2

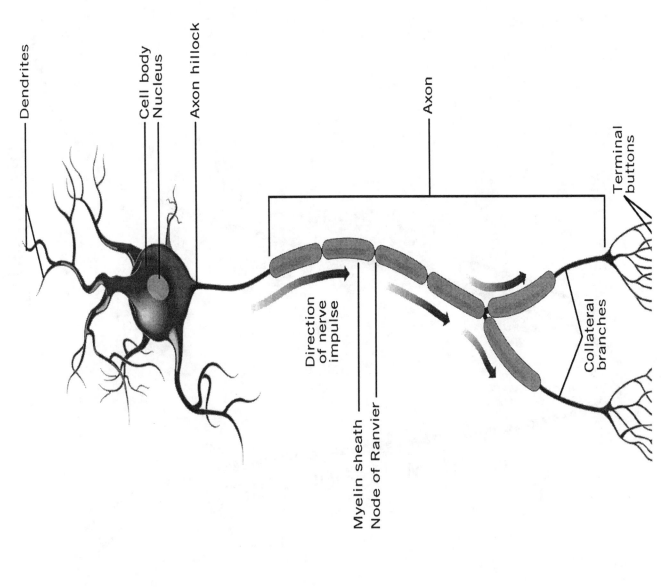

Dendrites

Cell body
Nucleus
Axon hillock

Axon

Direction
of nerve
impulse

Myelin sheath
Node of Ranvier

Collateral
branches

Terminal
buttons

Westen, 2e Fig. 3.1

15

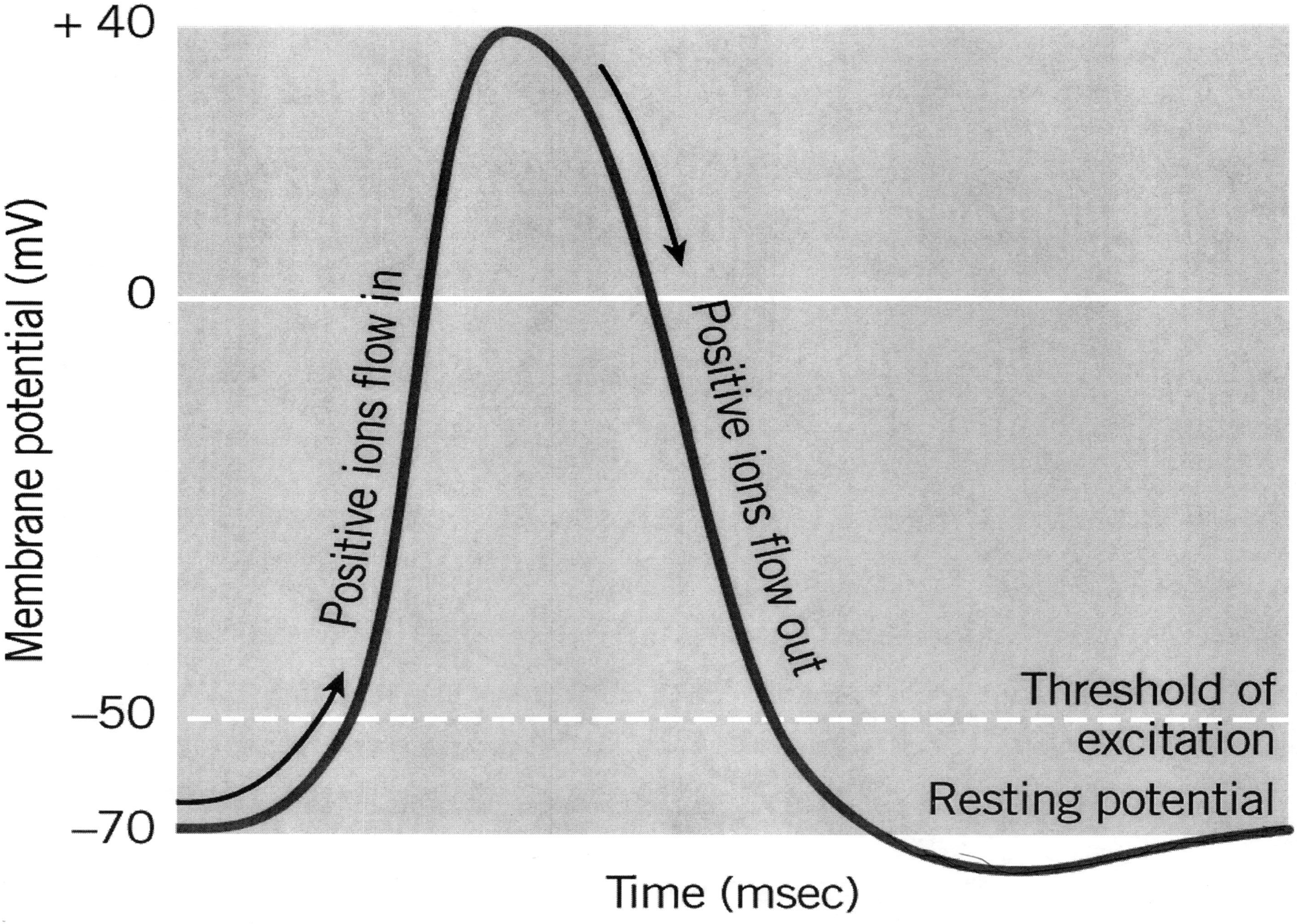

Positive ions flow out

Positive ions flow in

Threshold of excitation

Resting potential

Time (msec)

Membrane potential (mV)

+ 40

0

−50

−70

Westen, 2e Fig. 3.2

© 1999 John Wiley and Sons, Inc.

16

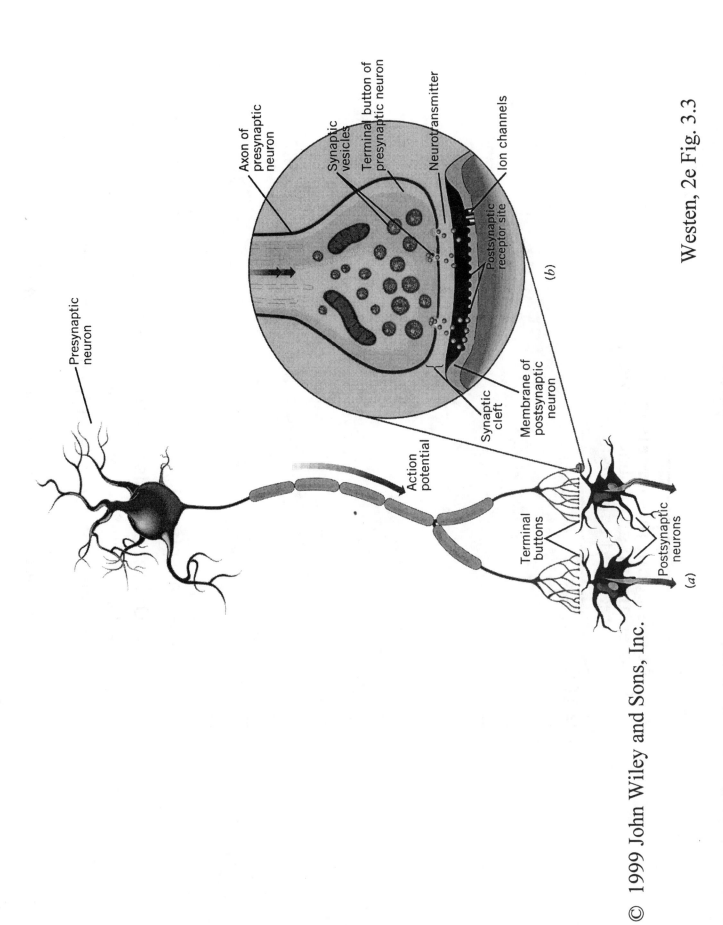

Presynaptic neuron

Axon of presynaptic neuron

Synaptic vesicles

Terminal button of presynaptic neuron

Neurotransmitter

Ion channels

Postsynaptic receptor site

Membrane of postsynaptic neuron

Synaptic cleft

Action potential

Terminal buttons

Postsynaptic neurons

(a)

(b)

Westen, 2e Fig. 3.3

At this point, the old rats in the experimental group had not yet received transplants.

Time 1 (before transplants)

Time 2 (after transplants)

Time taken to find submerged platform (sec)

— Old rat controls without transplants
— Old rats with transplants
— Young rat controls without transplants

(Figure adapted from Bjorklund & Gage, 1985)

Westen, 2e Fig. 3.4

© 1999 John Wiley and Sons, Inc.

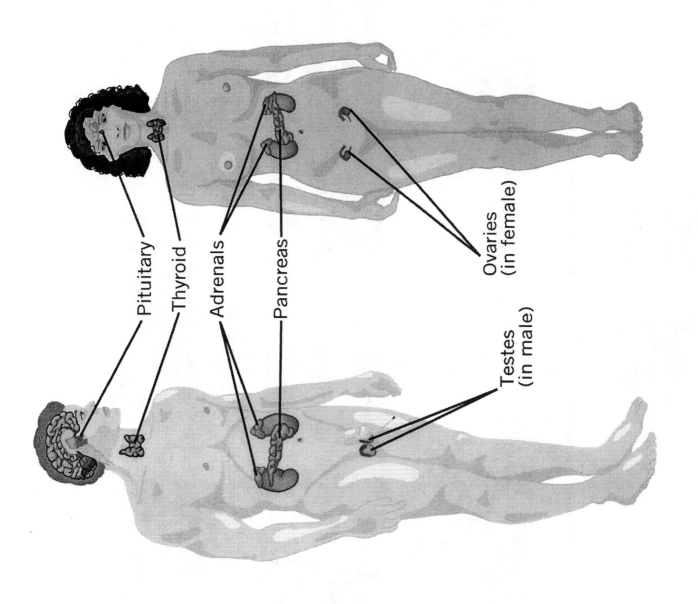

Pituitary

Thyroid

Adrenals

Pancreas

Ovaries
(in female)

Testes
(in male)

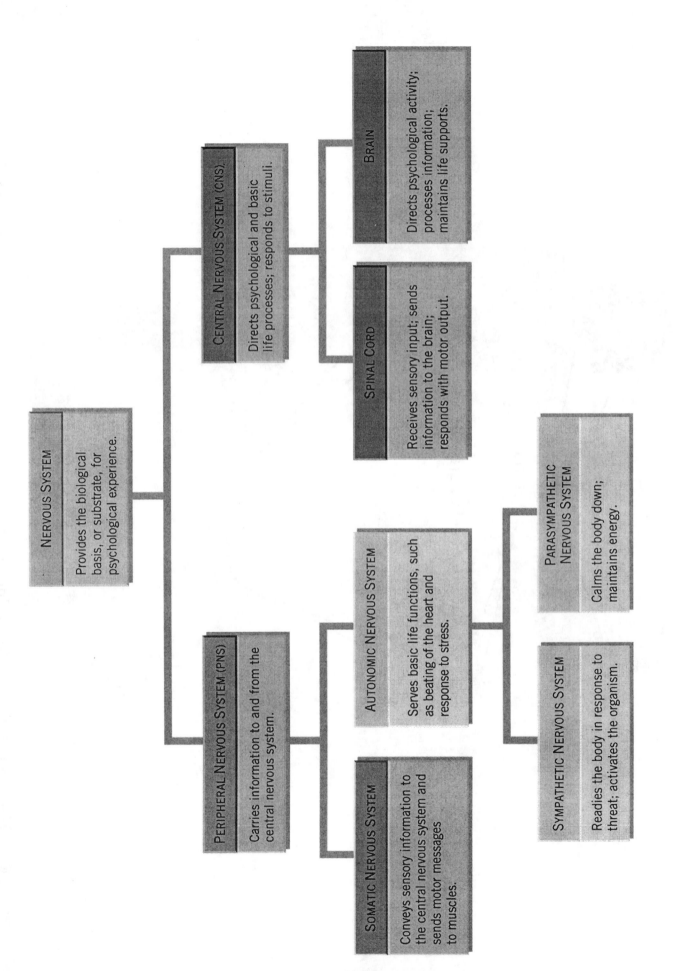

Westen, 2e Fig. 3.6

© 1999 John Wiley and Sons, Inc.

20

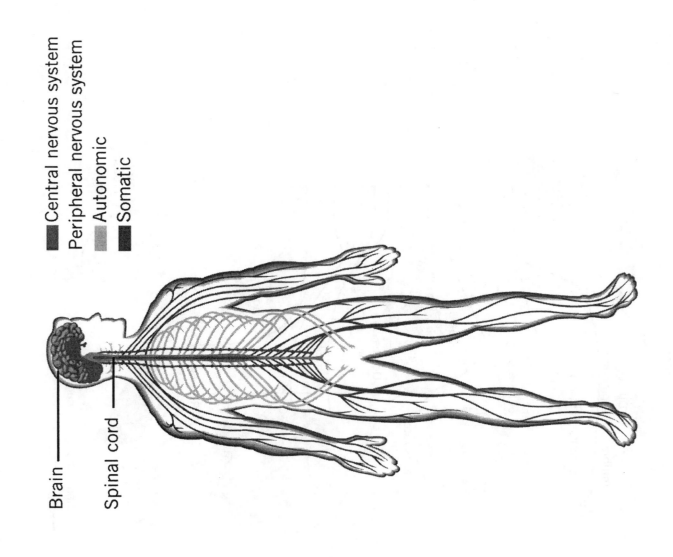

Central nervous system
Peripheral nervous system
Autonomic
Somatic

Brain

Spinal cord

Westen, 2e Fig. 3.7

© 1999 John Wiley and Sons, Inc.

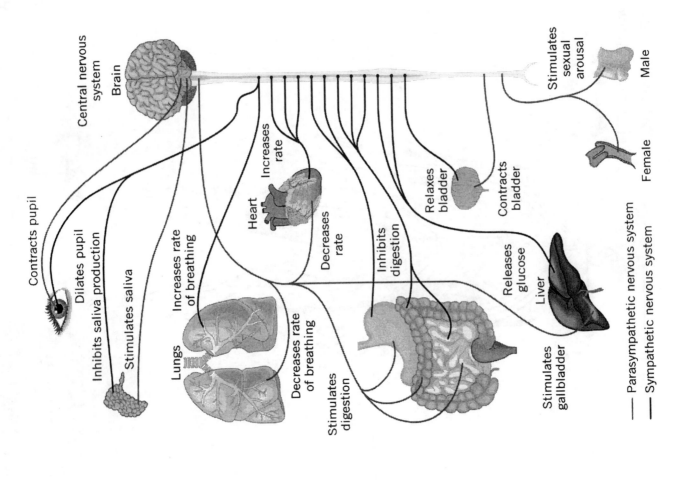

Central nervous system
Brain

Contracts pupil

Dilates pupil

Inhibits saliva production

Stimulates saliva

Increases rate of breathing

Lungs

Decreases rate of breathing

Stimulates digestion

Heart

Increases rate

Decreases rate

Inhibits digestion

Releases glucose

Liver

Stimulates gallbladder

Relaxes bladder

Contracts bladder

Stimulates sexual arousal

Male

Female

— Parasympathetic nervous system
— Sympathetic nervous system

Westen, 2e Fig. 3.8

© 1999 John Wiley and Sons, Inc.

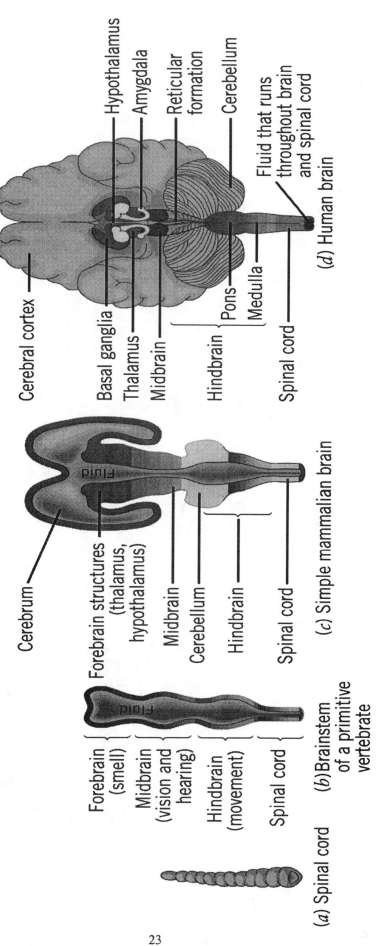

Cerebral cortex

Hypothalamus

Amygdala

Reticular formation

Cerebellum

Fluid that runs throughout brain and spinal cord

Basal ganglia

Thalamus

Midbrain

Pons

Medulla

Hindbrain

Spinal cord

(d) Human brain

Cerebrum

Forebrain structures (thalamus, hypothalamus)

Fluid

Midbrain

Cerebellum

Hindbrain

Spinal cord

(c) Simple mammalian brain

Forebrain (smell)

Midbrain (vision and hearing)

Hindbrain (movement)

Spinal cord

Fluid

(b) Brainstem of a primitive vertebrate

(a) Spinal cord

Westen, 2e Fig. 3.9

(Figure adapted from Kold & Wishaw, 1990)

© 1999 John Wiley and Sons, Inc.

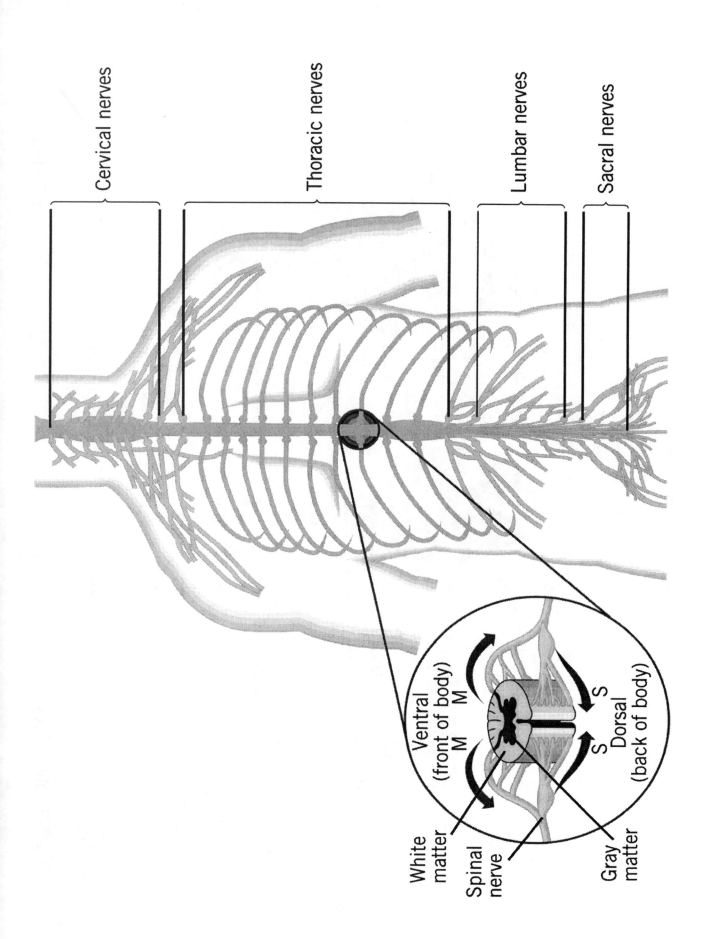

Cervical nerves

Thoracic nerves

Lumbar nerves

Sacral nerves

Ventral (front of body)
M M

S S
Dorsal (back of body)

White matter

Spinal nerve

Gray matter

Westen, 2e Fig. 3.10

© 1999 John Wiley and Sons, Inc.

24

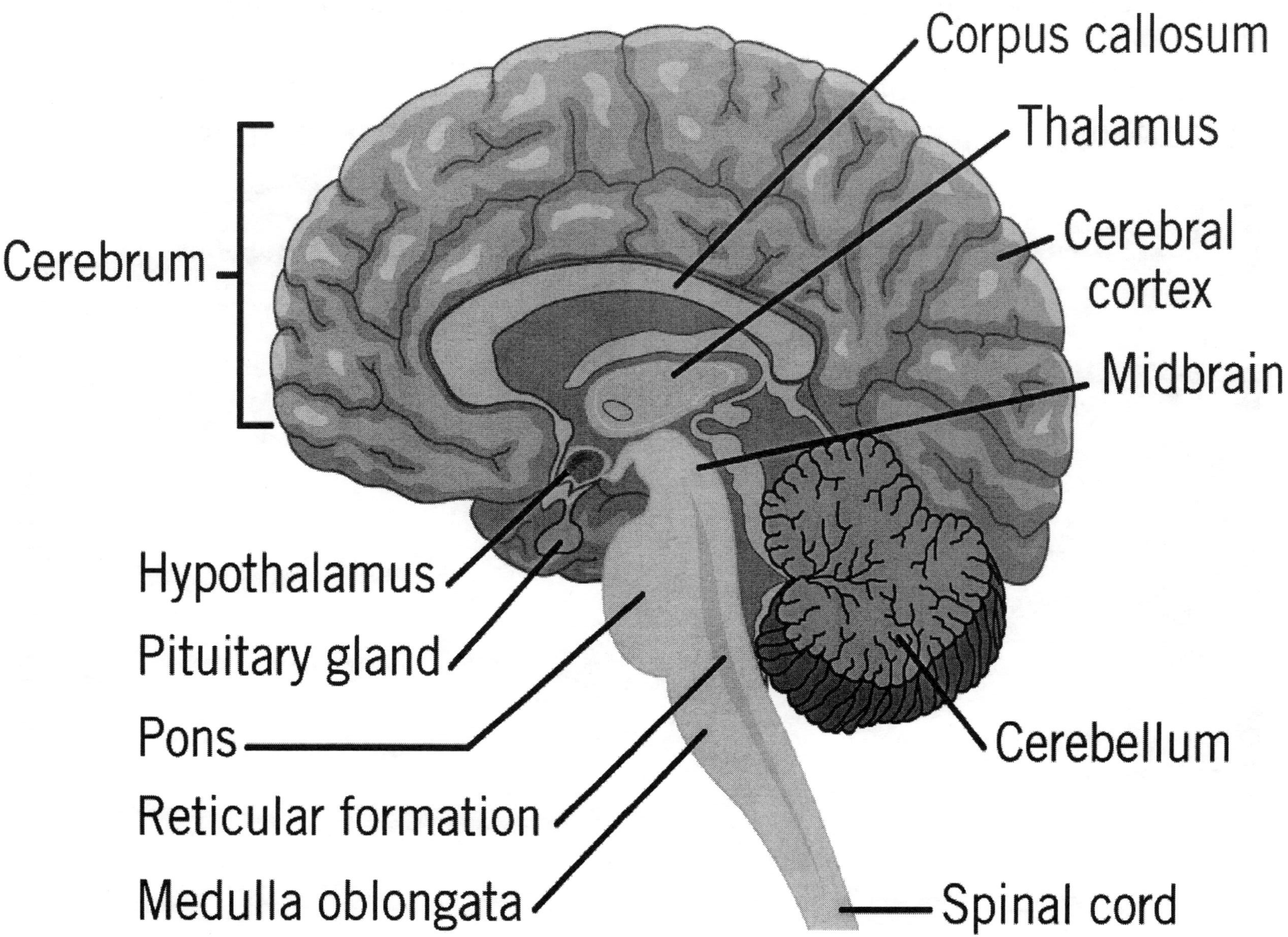

Corpus callosum
Thalamus
Cerebral cortex
Midbrain
Cerebellum
Spinal cord
Cerebrum
Hypothalamus
Pituitary gland
Pons
Reticular formation
Medulla oblongata

Westen, 2e Fig. 3.11

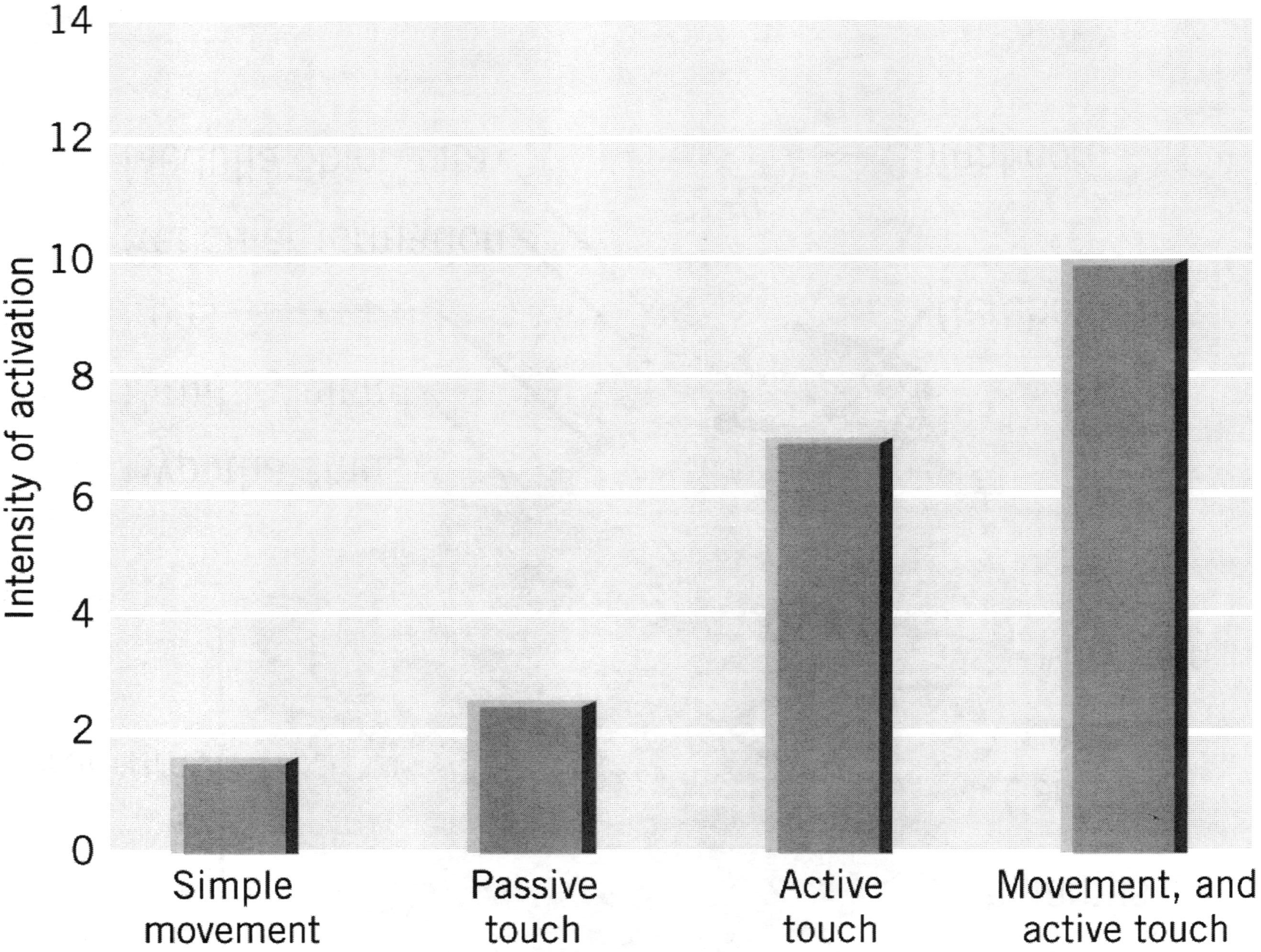

Intensity of activation

Simple movement

Passive touch

Active touch

Movement, and active touch

Westen, 2e Fig. 3.12

© 1999 John Wiley and Sons, Inc.

26

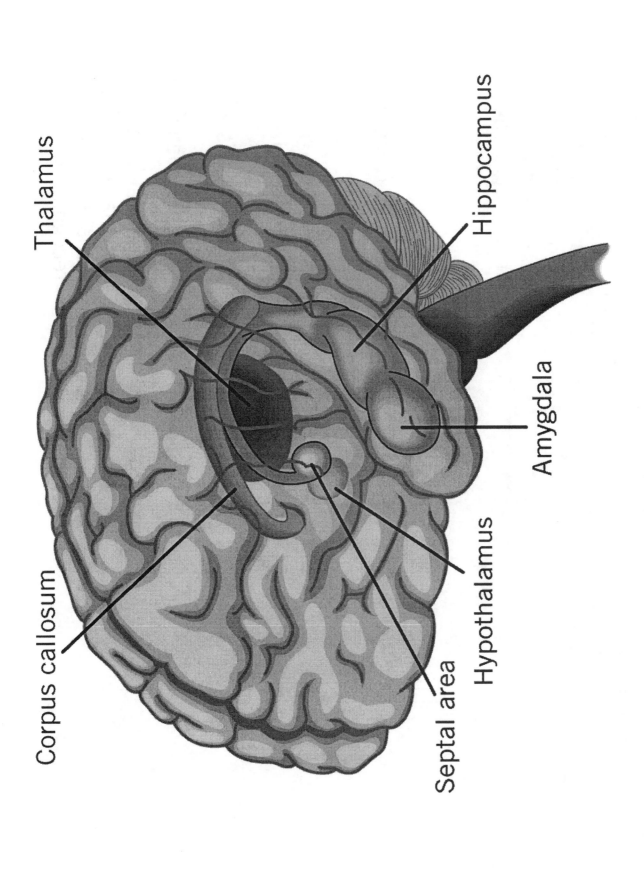

Thalamus

Hippocampus

Corpus callosum

Amygdala

Septal area

Hypothalamus

Westen, 2e Fig. 3.13

Central fissure

Somatosensory cortex

Parietal lobe (touch, spatial orientation, nonverbal thinking)

Occipital lobe (vision)

Primary visual cortex

Wernicke's area (speech comprehension)

Temporal lobe (language, hearing, visual pattern recognition)

Broca's area (speech production, grammar)

Motor cortex

Frontal lobe (abstract thinking, planning, social skills)

Westen, 2e Fig. 3.14

© 1999 John Wiley and Sons, Inc.

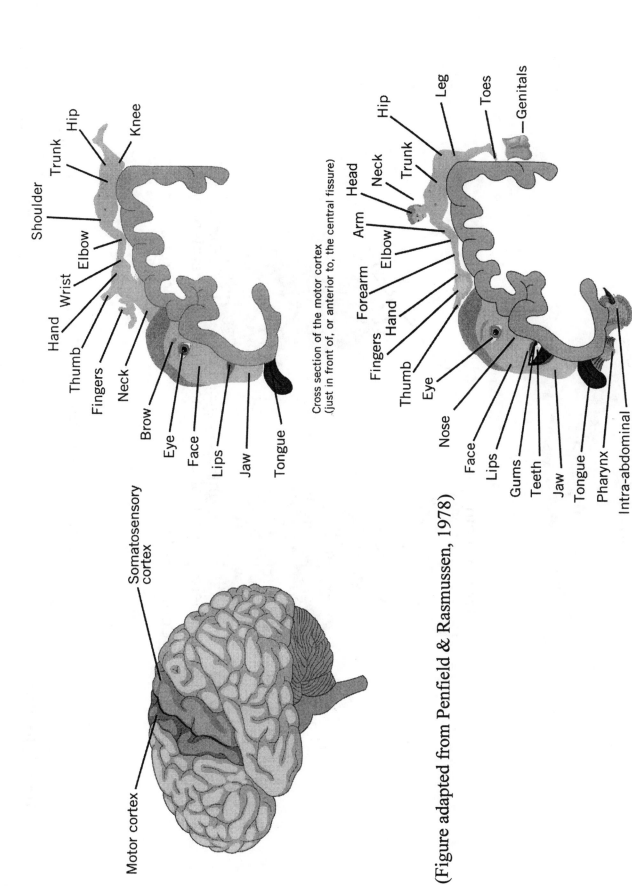

Shoulder
Trunk
Hip
Knee
Elbow
Wrist
Hand
Thumb
Fingers
Neck
Brow
Eye
Face
Lips
Jaw
Tongue

Cross section of the motor cortex
(just in front of, or anterior to, the central fissure)

Leg
Toes
Genitals
Hip
Head
Neck
Arm
Trunk
Forearm
Elbow
Hand
Fingers
Thumb
Eye
Nose
Face
Lips
Gums
Teeth
Jaw
Tongue
Pharynx
Intra-abdominal

Cross section of the somatosensory cortex
(just in behind, or posterior to, the central fissure)

Somatosensory cortex

Motor cortex

(Figure adapted from Penfield & Rasmussen, 1978)

Westen, 2e Fig. 3.15

© 1999 John Wiley and Sons, Inc.

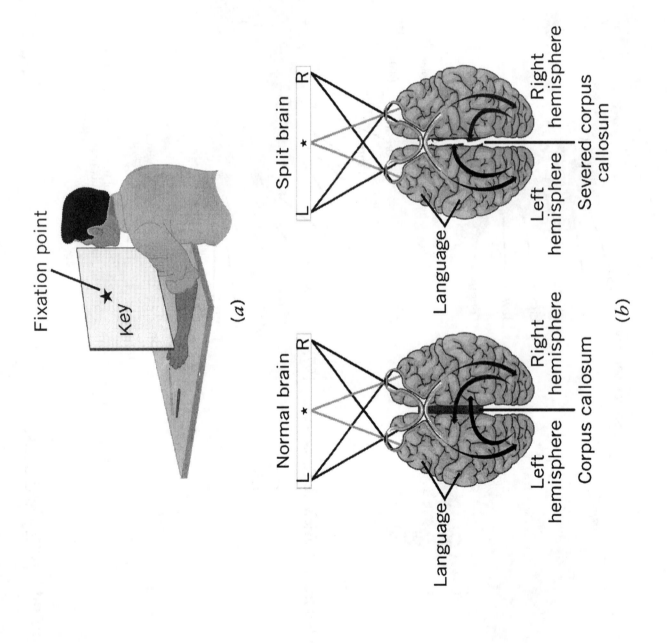

Fixation point

Key

(a)

Normal brain

Language

R

L

★

Left hemisphere   Right hemisphere

Corpus callosum

Split brain

Language

R

L

★

Left hemisphere   Right hemisphere

Severed corpus callosum

(b)

(Figure adapted from Gazzaniga, 1967)

Westen, 2e Fig. 3.16

© 1999 John Wiley and Sons, Inc.

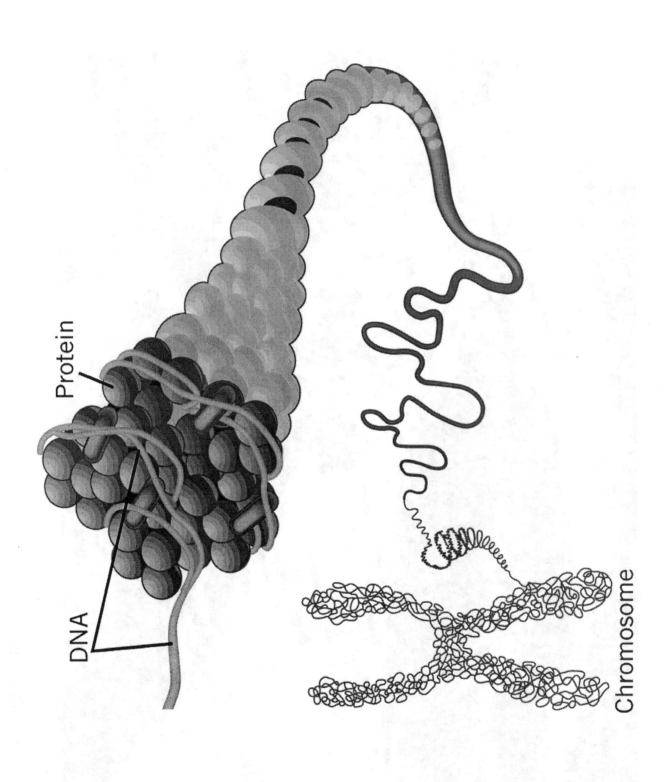

Protein

DNA

Chromosome

Westen, 2e Fig. 3.18

© 1999 John Wiley and Sons, Inc.

(Figure adapted from Sekuler & Blake, 1994, pp. 28-29)

Westen, 2e Fig. 4.2

© 1999 John Wiley and Sons, Inc.

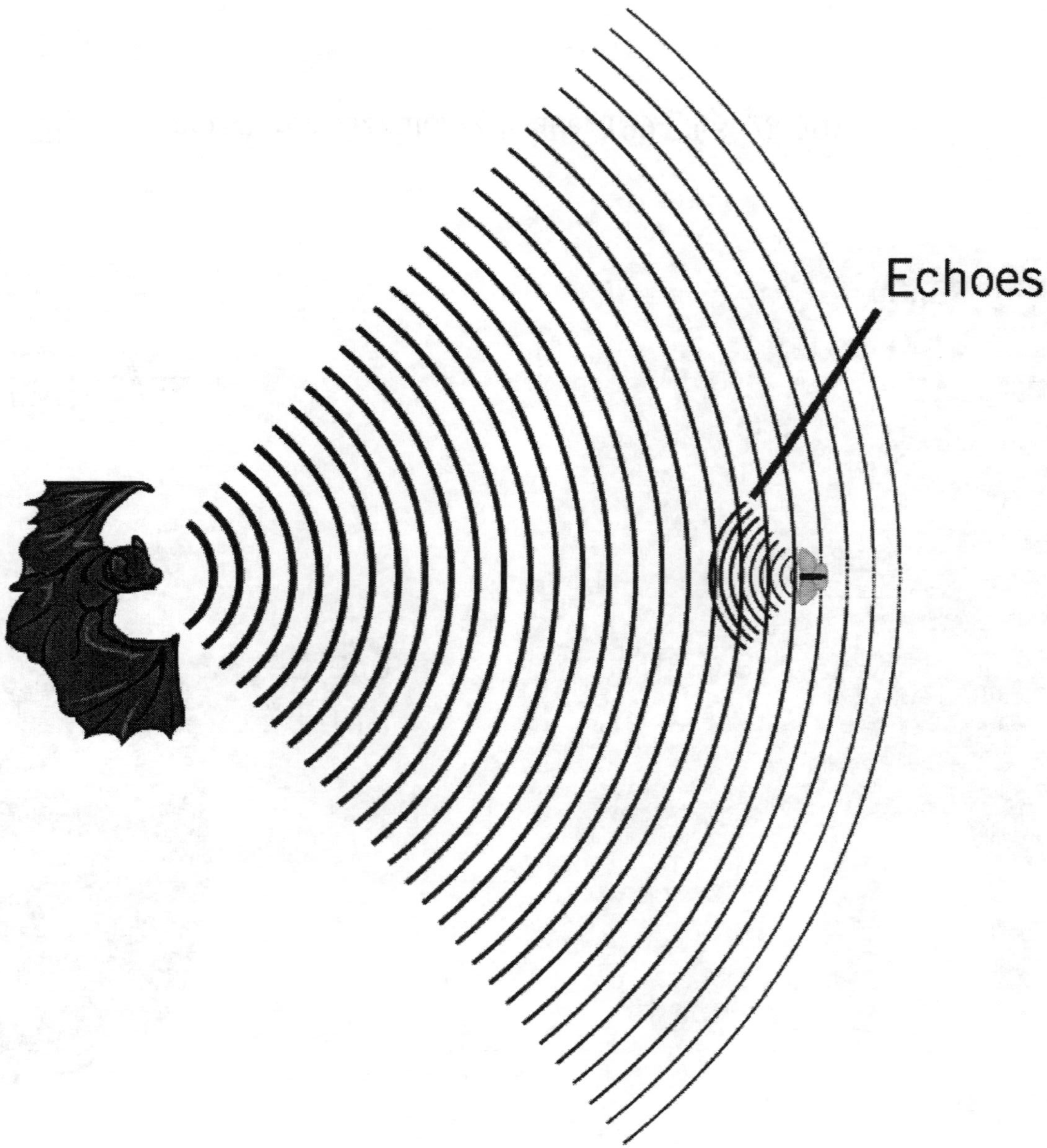

Echoes

(Figure adapted from Griffin, 1959, p. 86)

Westen, 2e Fig. 4.3

© 1999 John Wiley and Sons, Inc.

Note that at high stimulus intensities, a "no" response bias does not appreciably diminish the number of hits because presence or absence of stimulation is so obvious.

Bias toward responding "yes"

Sensitivity

Bias toward responding "no"

Proportions of hits

Proportions of false alarms

(c) ROC curve

CONDITION	SUBJECT'S RESPONSE	
	"Yes"	"No"
Stimulus presented	+ $1.00 (small gain)	– $1.00 (small loss)
Stimulus not presented	– $10.00 (large loss)	+ $10.00 (large gain)

(b) Matrix that will produce a "no" bias

CONDITION	SUBJECT'S RESPONSE	
	"Yes"	"No"
Stimulus presented	+ $10.00 (large gain)	– $10.00 (large loss)
Stimulus not presented	– $1.00 (small loss)	+ $1.00 (small gain)

(a) Matrix that will produce a "yes" bias

Westen, 2e Fig. 4.4

© 1999 John Wiley and Sons, Inc.

35

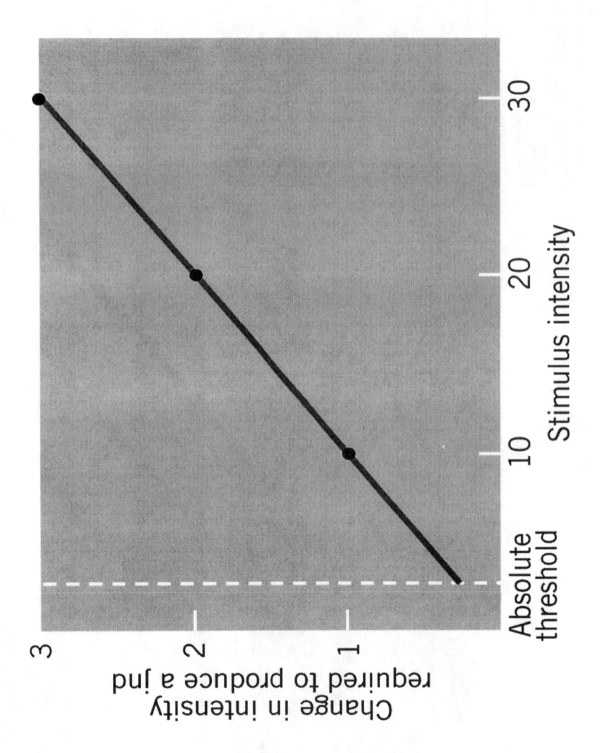

Change in intensity required to produce a jnd

Stimulus intensity

Absolute threshold

(Figure adapted from Guilford, 1954, p. 38)

Westen, 2e Fig. 4.5

© 1999 John Wiley and Sons, Inc.

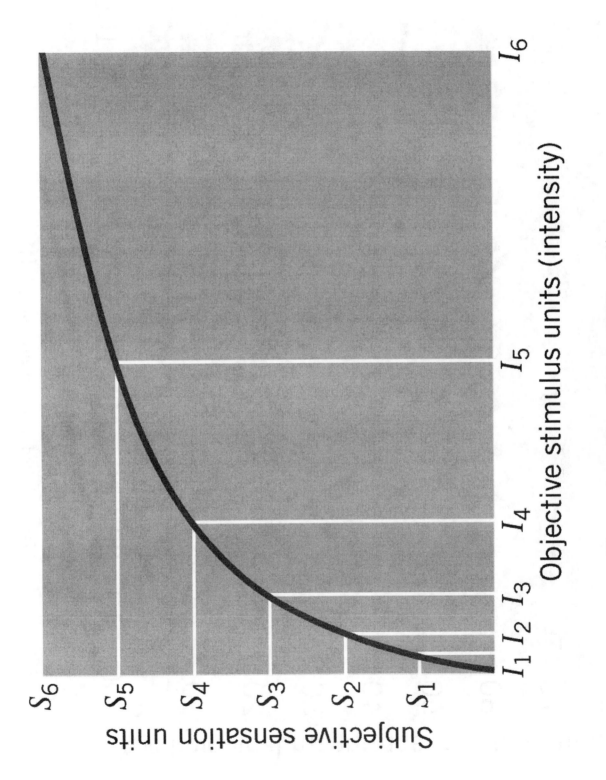

Objective stimulus units (intensity)

Subjective sensation units

I_1 I_2 I_3 I_4 I_5 I_6

S_1 S_2 S_3 S_4 S_5 S_6

(Figure adapted from Stevens, 1961, p. 11)

Westen, 2e Fig. 4.5b

© 1999 John Wiley and Sons, Inc.

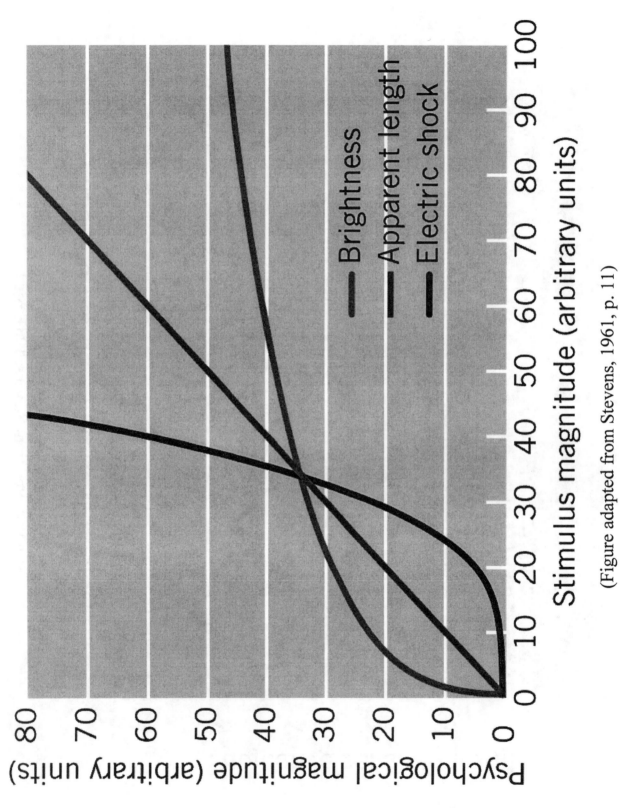

Psychological magnitude (arbitrary units)

Stimulus magnitude (arbitrary units)

— Brightness
— Apparent length
— Electric shock

(Figure adapted from Stevens, 1961, p. 11)

Westen, 2e Fig. 4.5c

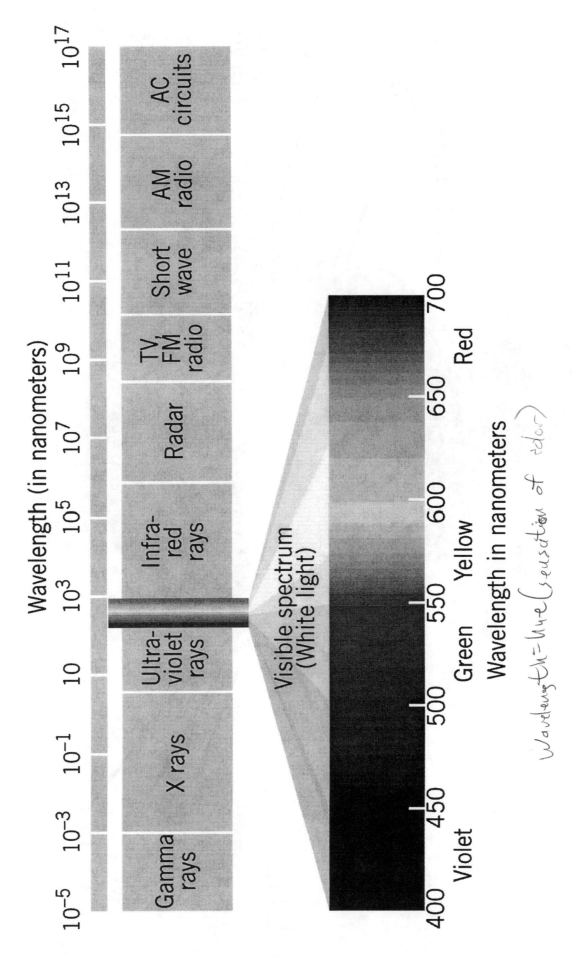

© 1999 John Wiley and Sons, Inc.

Westen, 2e Fig. 4.6

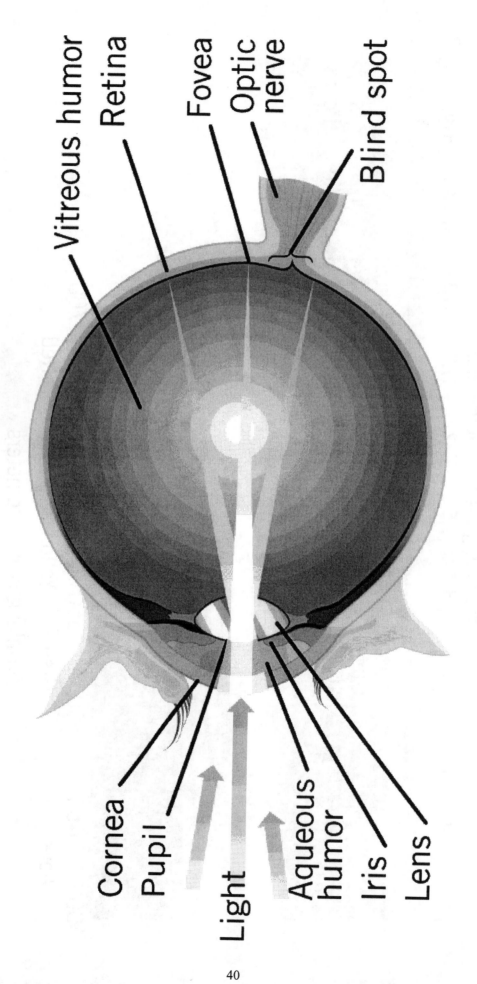

Vitreous humor
Retina
Fovea
Optic nerve
Blind spot

Cornea
Pupil
Light
Aqueous humor
Iris
Lens

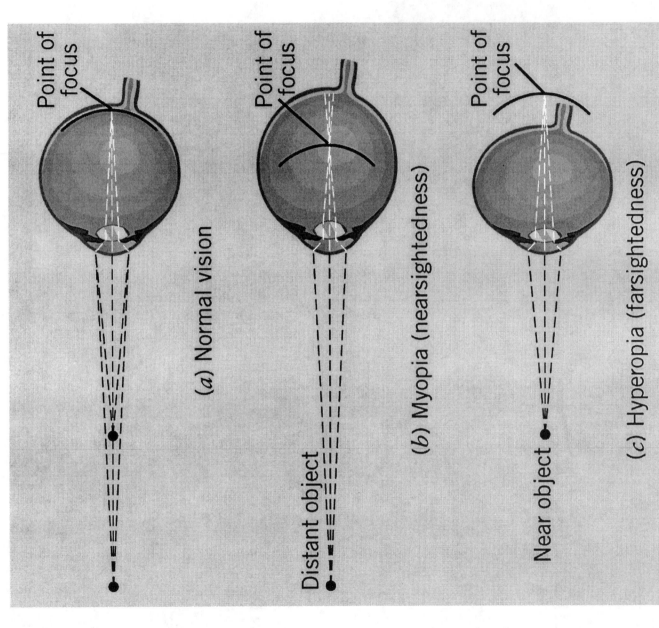

(a) Normal vision

(b) Myopia (nearsightedness)

(c) Hyperopia (farsightedness)

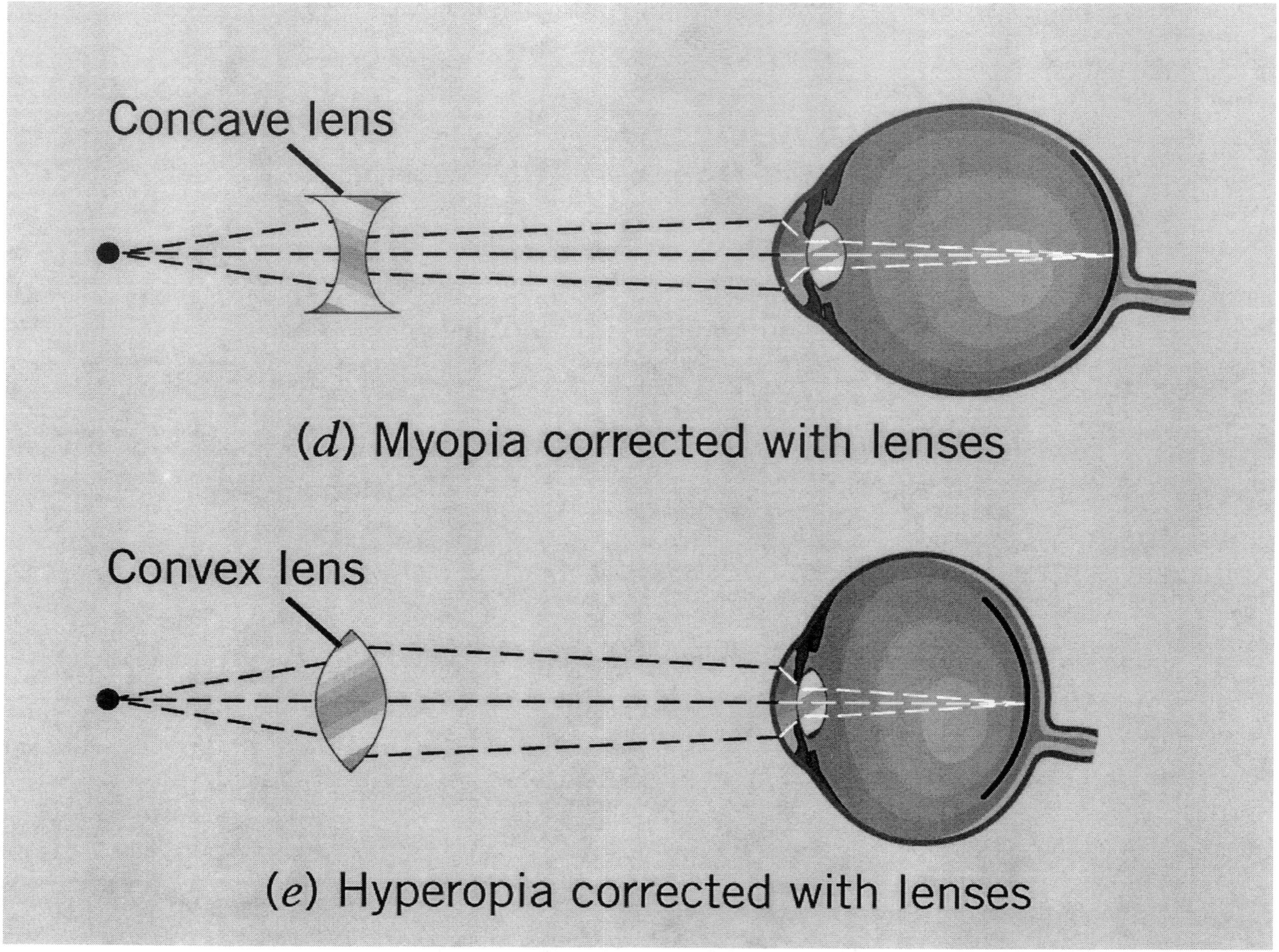

Concave lens

(d) Myopia corrected with lenses

Convex lens

(e) Hyperopia corrected with lenses

Light

Retina

Ganglion
cell axons

Ganglion cells

Bipolar cells

Rod

Cone

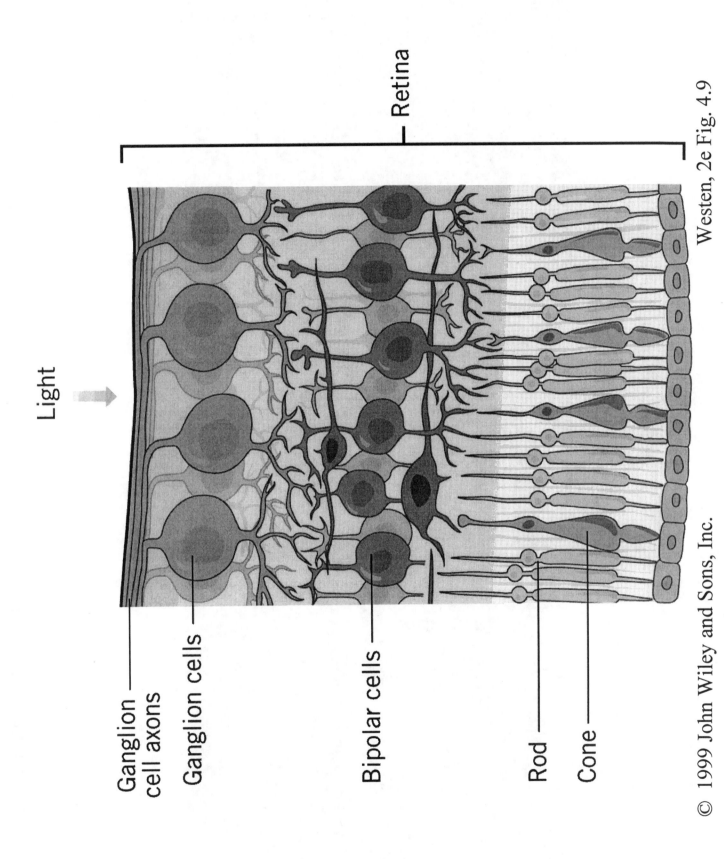

Westen, 2e Fig. 4.9

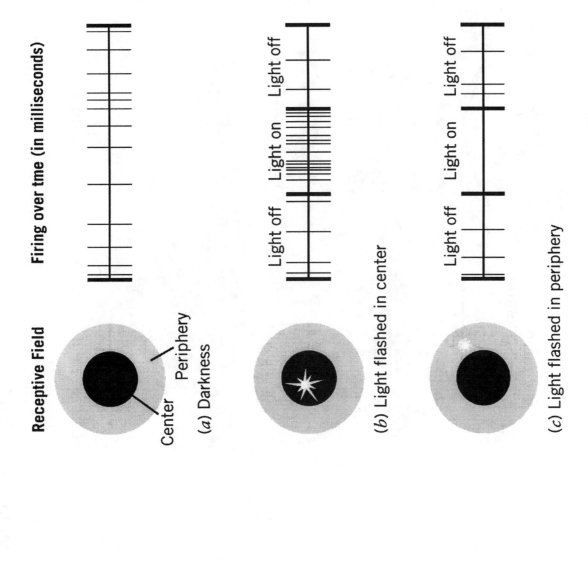

Receptive Field　　**Firing over tme (in milliseconds)**

Center　Periphery

(a) Darkness

Light off　　Light on　　Light off

(b) Light flashed in center

Light off　　Light on　　Light off

(c) Light flashed in periphery

(Figure adapted from Sekuler & Blake, 1994, p. 68)

Westen, 2e Fig. 4.11

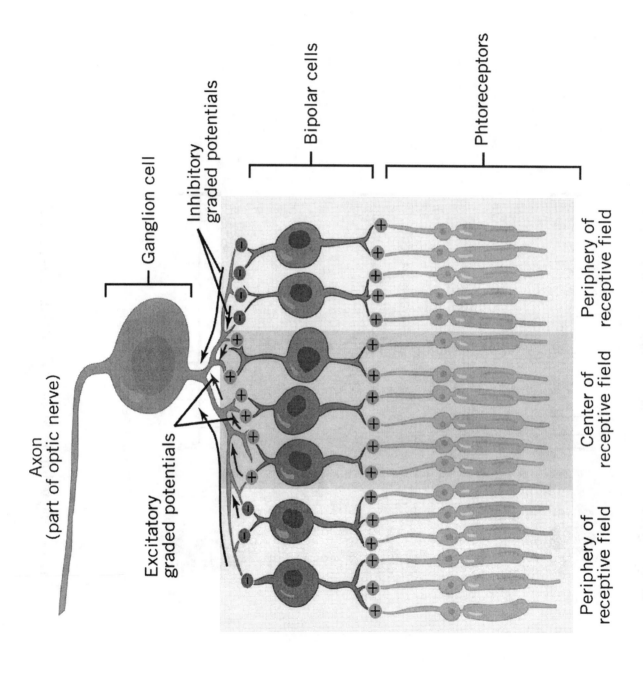

Ganglion cell

Axon
(part of optic nerve)

Inhibitory
graded potentials

Excitatory
graded potentials

Bipolar cells

Phtoreceptors

Periphery of
receptive field

Center of
receptive field

Periphery of
receptive field

Westen, 2e Fig. 4.12

© 1999 John Wiley and Sons, Inc.

Westen, 2e Fig. 4.13

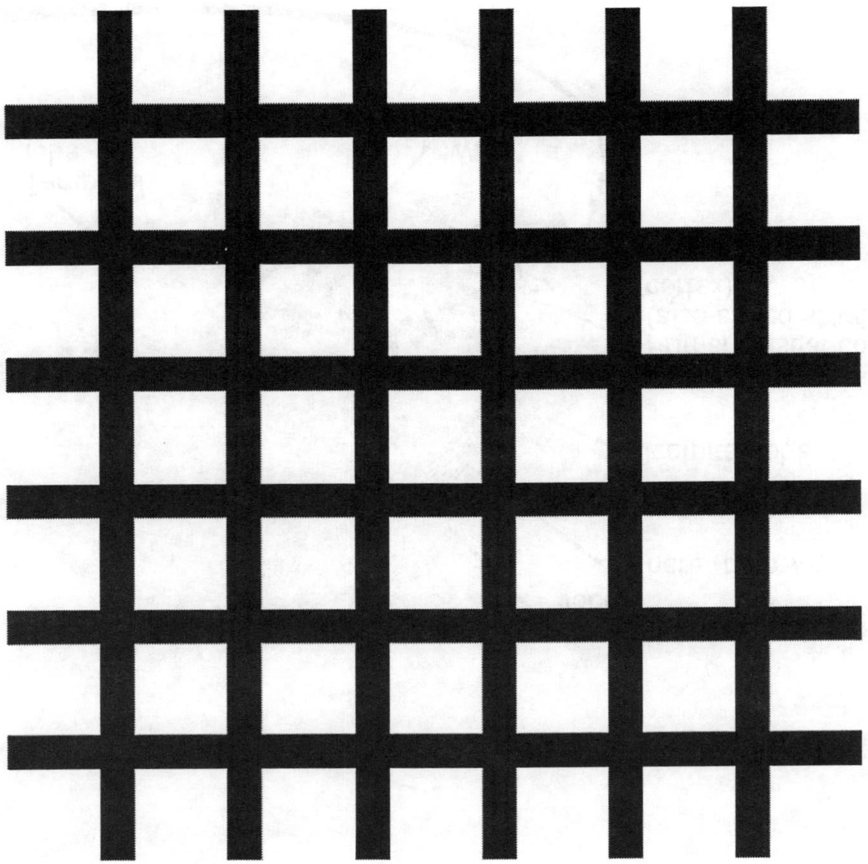

(b)

(a)

Left visual field · Right visual field

Right eye · Optic nerve · Optic chiasm · Optic tract

Left eye · Retina

Visual association cortex · Primary visual cortex

Lateral geniculate nucleus · Superior colliculus · Neural fibers projecting to occipital lobes

(a)

Parietal lobe · "Where" pathway · Occipital lobe · Primary visual cortex (also called striate cortex)

"What" pathway

Temporal lobe

(b)

Westen, 2e Fig. 4.14

© 1999 John Wiley and Sons, Inc.

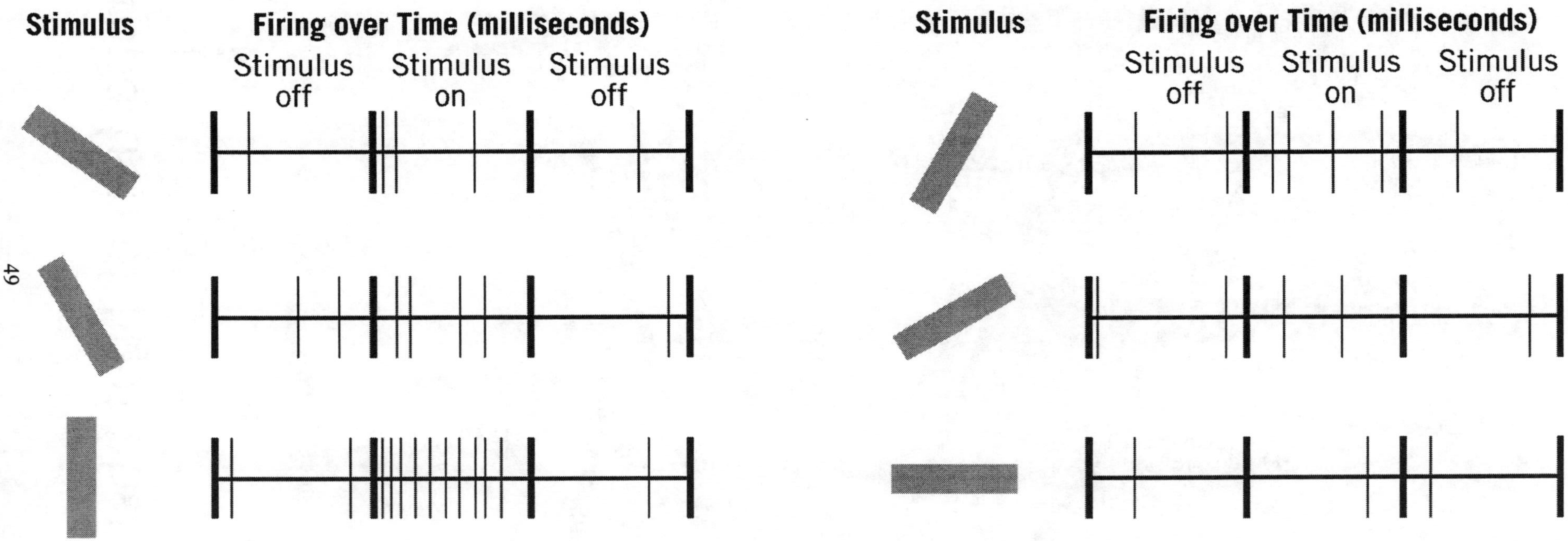

Stimulus

Firing over Time (milliseconds)

Stimulus off   Stimulus on   Stimulus off

(Figure adapted from Sekuler & Blake, 1994, p. 119)

Westen, 2e Fig. 4.15

© 1999 John Wiley and Sons, Inc.

49

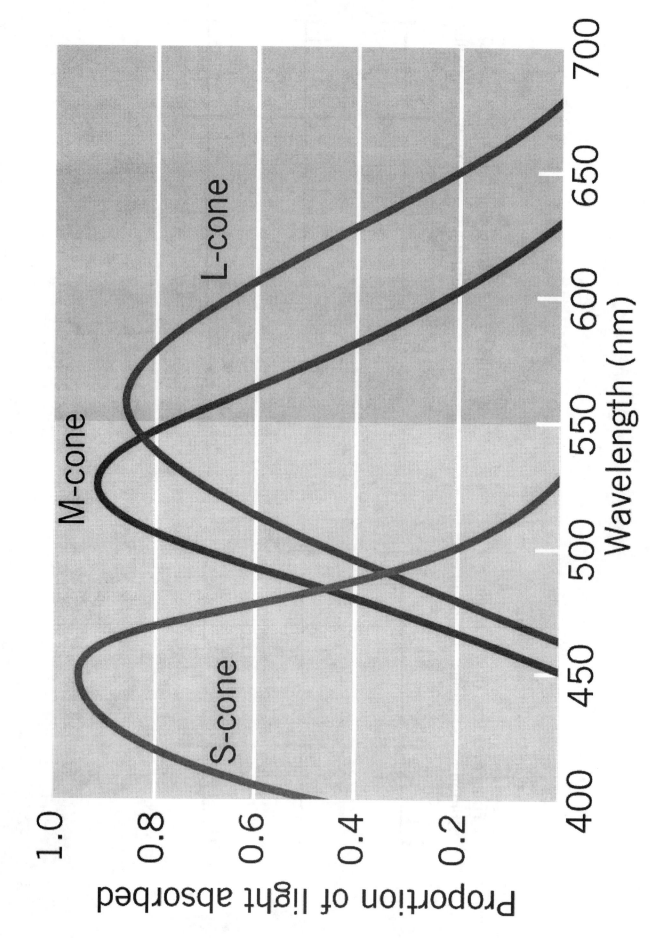

Proportion of light absorbed

Wavelength (nm)

M-cone

S-cone

L-cone

Westen, 2e Fig. 4.16

© 1999 John Wiley and Sons, Inc.

50

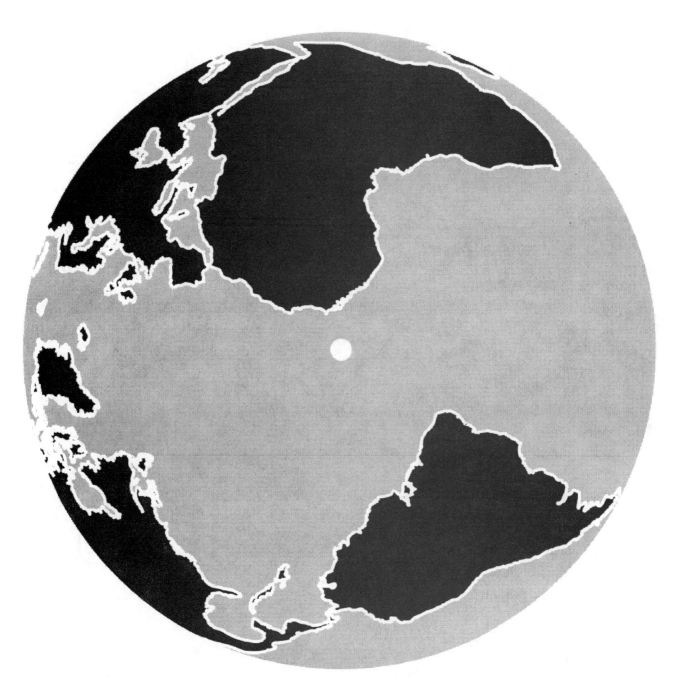

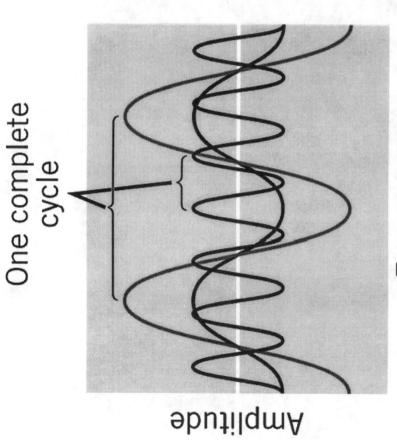

One complete cycle

Amplitude

Frequency

— High frequency, low amplitude (soft tenor or soprano)

— Low frequency, low amplitude (soft bass)

— Low frequency, high amplitude (loud bass)

Westen, 2e Fig. 4.19

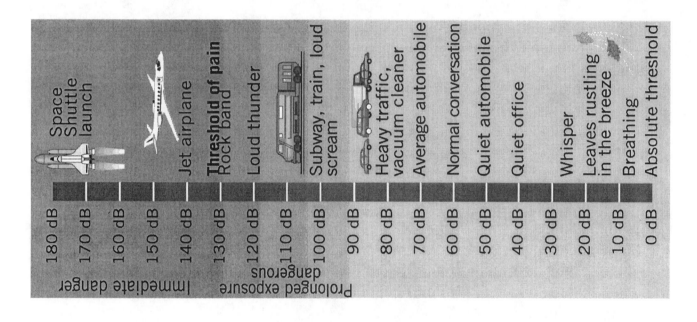

180 dB	Space Shuttle launch
170 dB	
160 dB	
150 dB	Jet airplane
140 dB	
130 dB	**Threshold of pain** Rock band
120 dB	Loud thunder
110 dB	
100 dB	Subway, train, loud scream
90 dB	
80 dB	Heavy traffic, vacuum cleaner
70 dB	Average automobile
60 dB	Normal conversation
50 dB	Quiet automobile
40 dB	Quiet office
30 dB	Whisper
20 dB	Leaves rustling in the breeze
10 dB	Breathing
0 dB	Absolute threshold

Immediate danger

Prolonged exposure dangerous

Westen, 2e Fig. 4.20

© 1999 John Wiley and Sons, Inc.

Oval window (under stapes)

Auditory nerve

Cochlea

Eustachian tube

Vesticular sacs

Inner ear

Semicircular canals

Middle ear

Stapes (stirrup)

Incus (anvil)

Ossicles

Malleus (hammer)

Outer ear

Round window

Ear drum (tympanic membrane)

Pinna

Auditory canal

Westen, 2e Fig. 4.21

© 1999 John Wiley and Sons, Inc.

Vestibular canal

Cochlear duct

Basilar membrane

Oval window

Stapes (stirrup)

Tympanic canal

(a)

Stapes (stirrup)

Oval window

Tectorial membrane

Hair cells

Organ of Corti

Cochlear duct

Basilar membrane

Vestibular canal

Tympanic canal

(b)

Auditory nerve

Round window

Westen, 2e Fig. 4.22

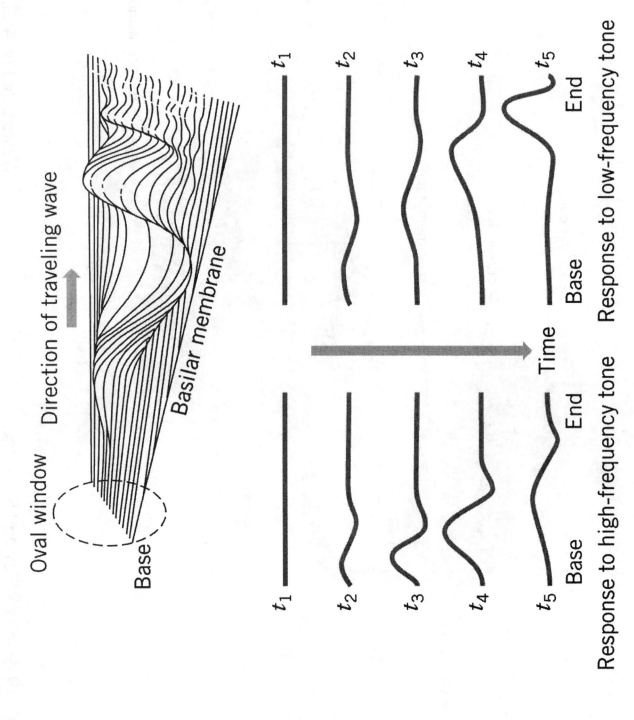

Oval window
Direction of traveling wave
Basilar membrane
Base

t_1
t_2
t_3
t_4
t_5
End

Base
Response to low-frequency tone

Time

t_1
t_2
t_3
t_4
t_5
Base   End

Response to high-frequency tone

(Figure adapted from Sekuler & Blake, 1994, p. 315)

Westen, 2e Fig. 4.23

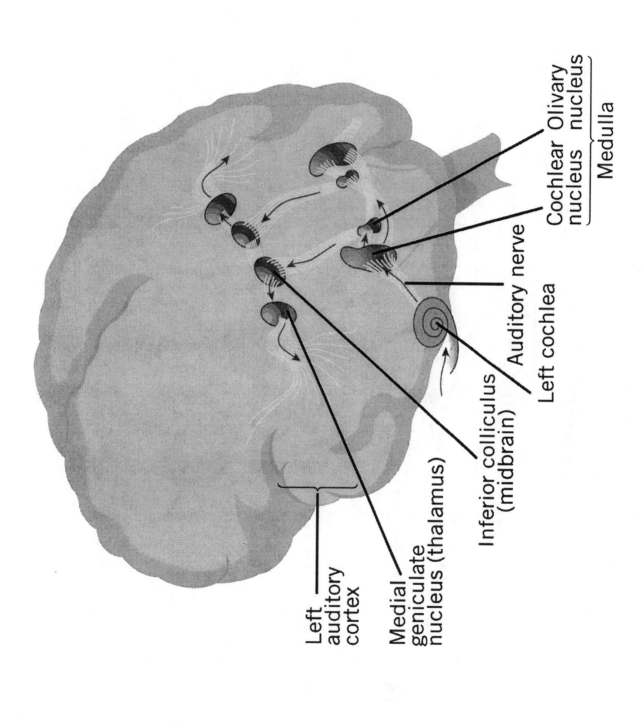

Left auditory cortex

Medial geniculate nucleus (thalamus)

Inferior colliculus (midbrain)

Left cochlea

Auditory nerve

Cochlear nucleus

Olivary nucleus

Medulla

Westen, 2e Fig. 4.24

© 1999 John Wiley and Sons, Inc.

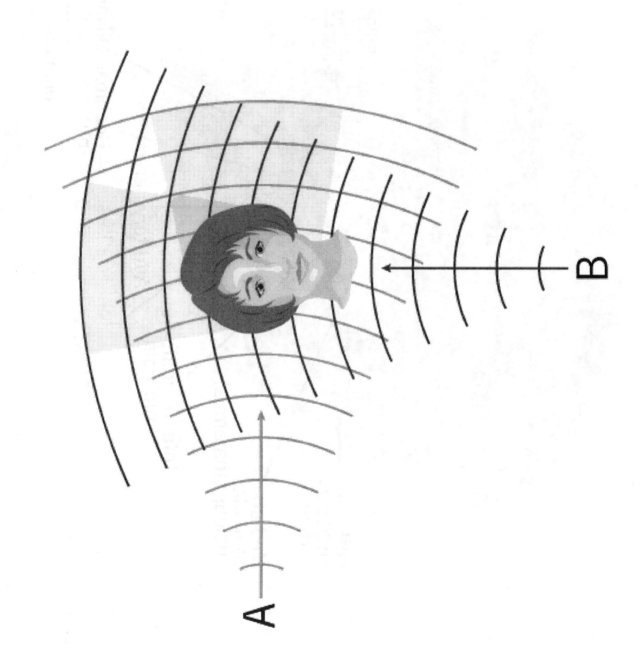

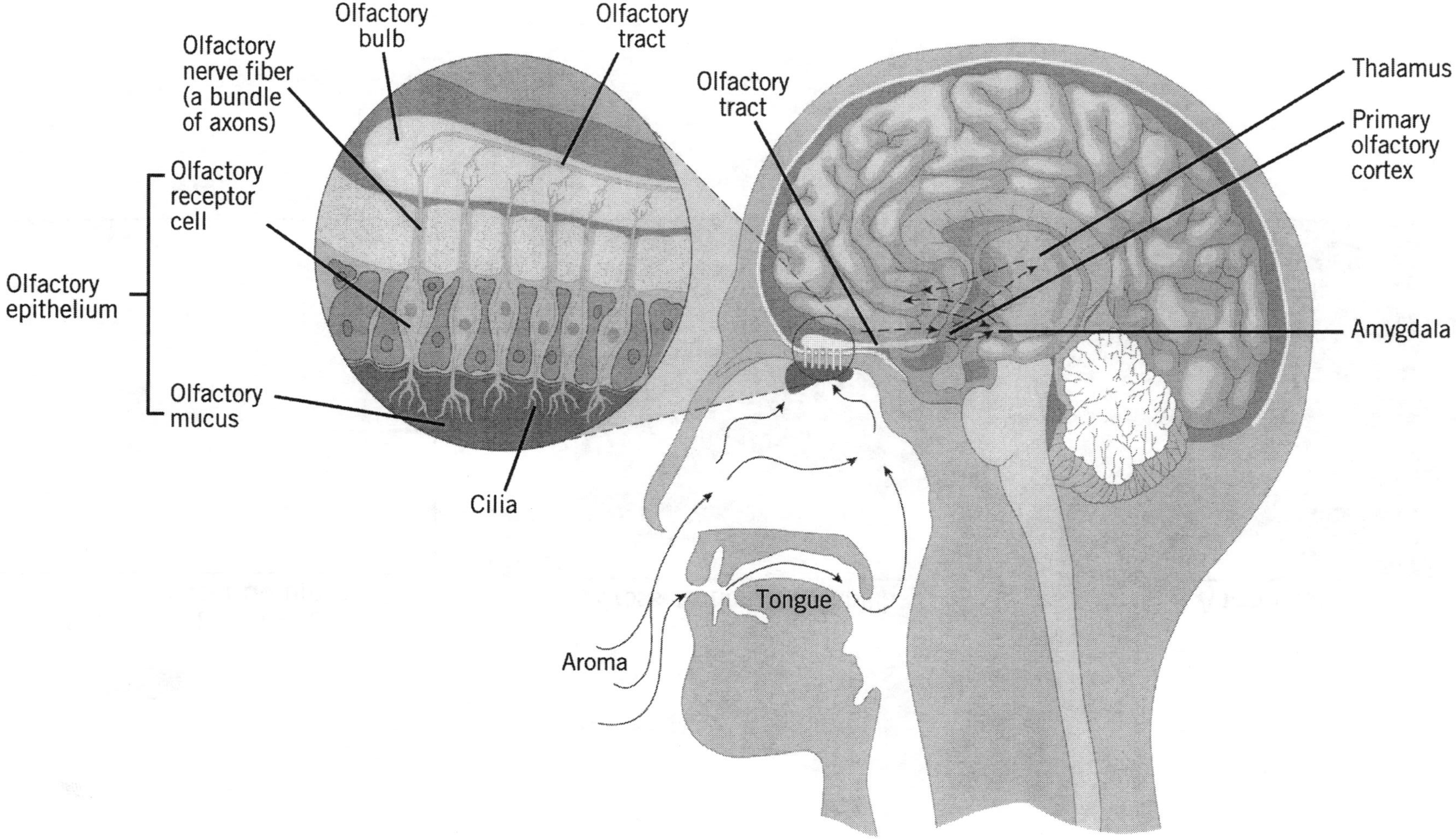

Thalamus

Primary olfactory cortex

Amygdala

Olfactory tract

Olfactory tract

Olfactory bulb

Olfactory nerve fiber (a bundle of axons)

Olfactory receptor cell

Olfactory epithelium

Olfactory mucus

Cilia

Tongue

Aroma

Westen, 2e Fig. 4.26

© 1999 John Wiley and Sons, Inc.

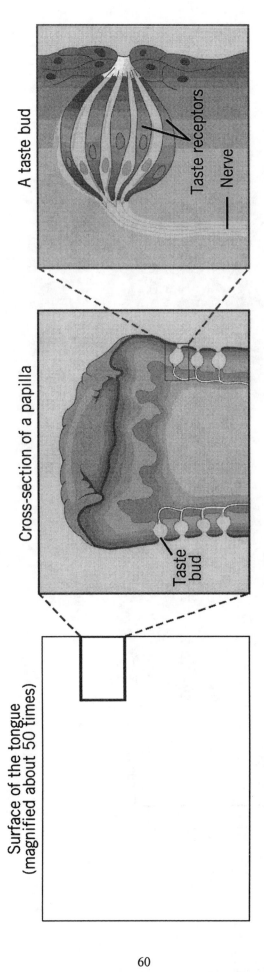

A taste bud

Taste receptors

Nerve

Cross-section of a papilla

Taste bud

Surface of the tongue
(magnified about 50 times)

Westen, 2e Fig. 4.27

© 1999 John Wiley and Sons, Inc.

Skin receptors

Outer layer of skin
Meissner's corpuscle
Merkel's disk
Free nerve ending
Krause's end-bulb
Pacinian corpuscle
Nerve ending around hair follicle

Hair shaft

Westen, 2e Fig. 4.28

© 1999 John Wiley and Sons, Inc.

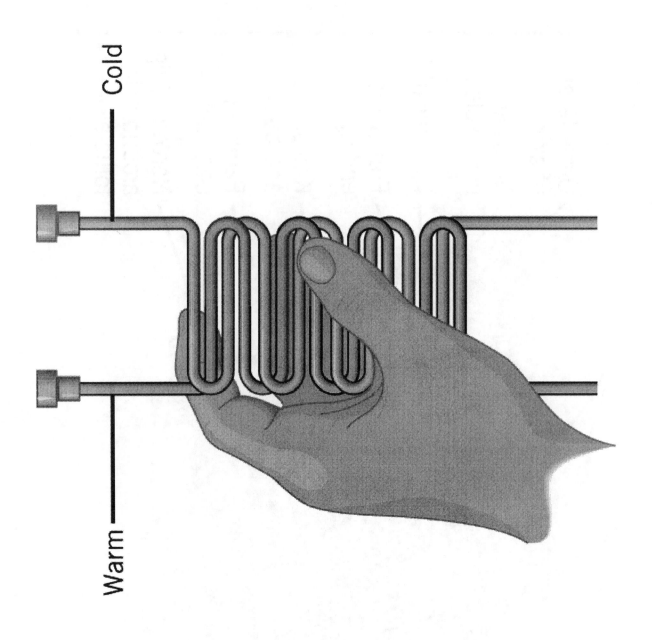

Cold

Warm

(Figure adapted from Boring, 1930, p. 42)

Westen, 2e Fig. 4.30

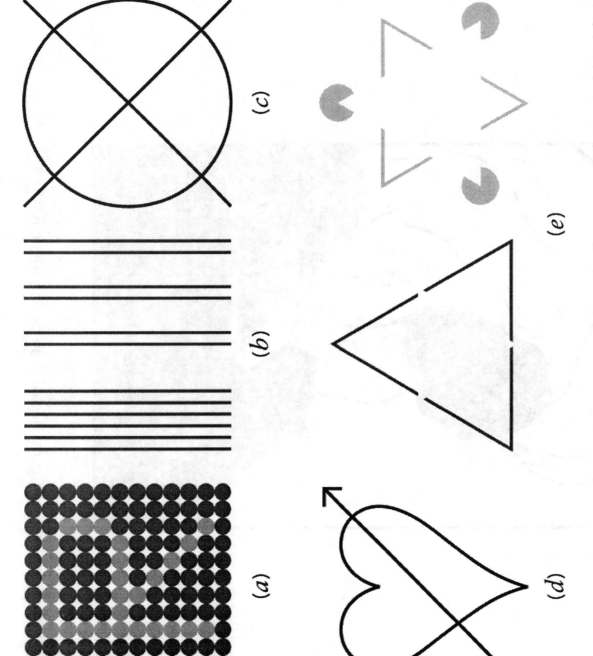

(a)

(b)

(c)

(d)

(e)

(Figure e adapted from Kanizsa, 1976)

Westen, 2e Fig. 4.30

© 1999 John Wiley and Sons, Inc.

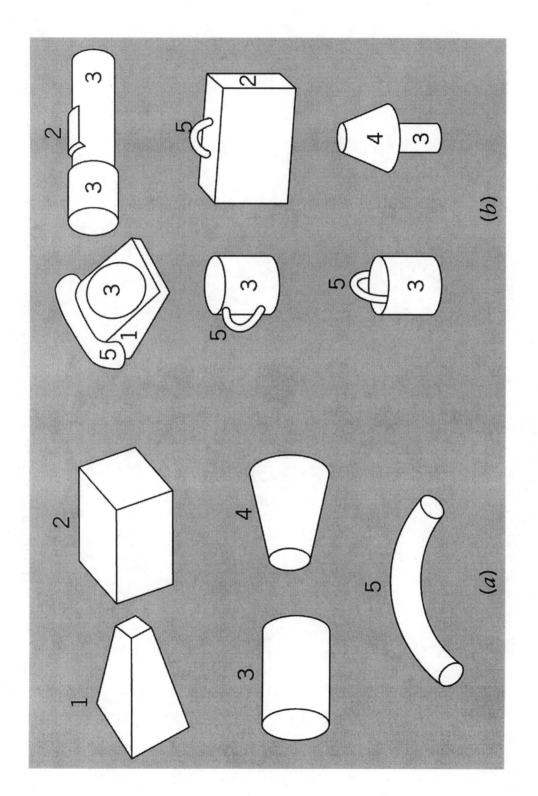

(Figure adapted from Biederman, 1990, p. 49)

Westen, 2e Fig. 4.32

(Figure adapted from Biederman, 1987, p. 135)

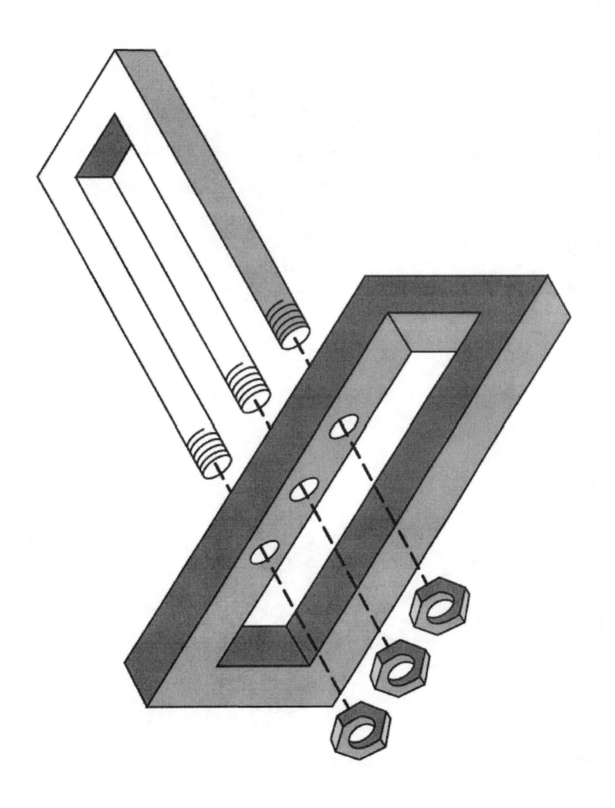

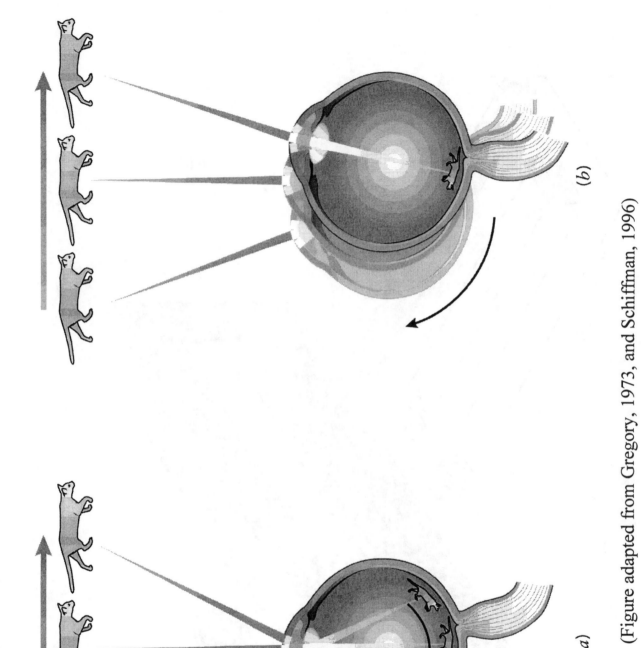

(a)

(b)

(Figure adapted from Gregory, 1973, and Schiffman, 1996)

Westen, 2e Fig. 4.37

© 1999 John Wiley and Sons, Inc.

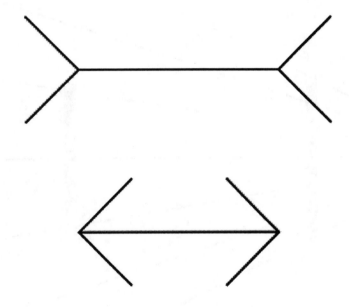

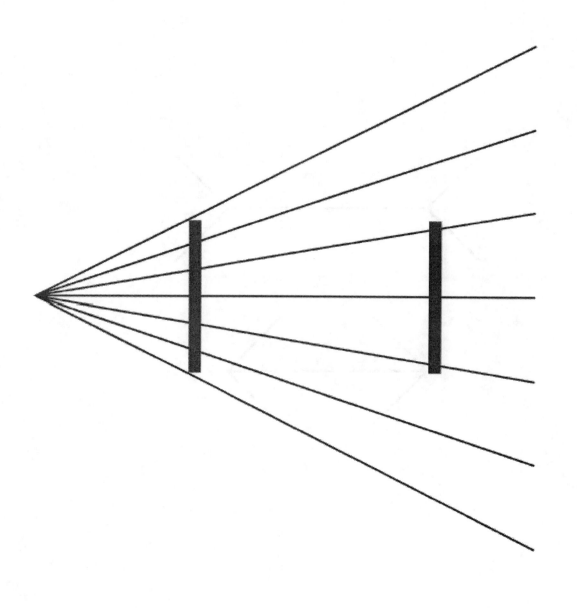

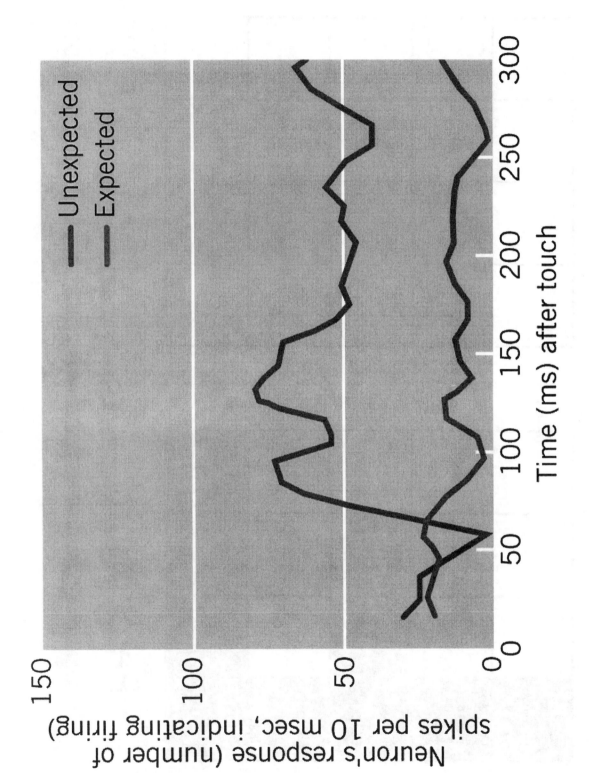

(Figure adapted from Mistlin & Perrerr, 1990)

Westen, 2e Fig. 4.44

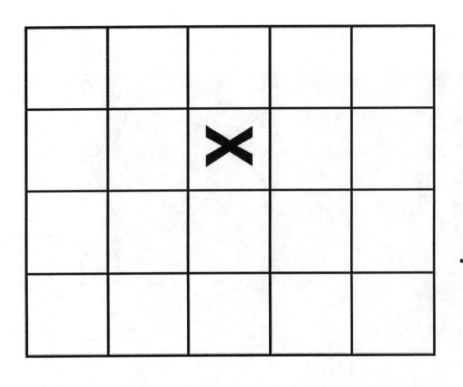

Imagery

Perception

Westen, 2e Fig. 4.45

© 1999 John Wiley and Sons, Inc.

(a)

(b)

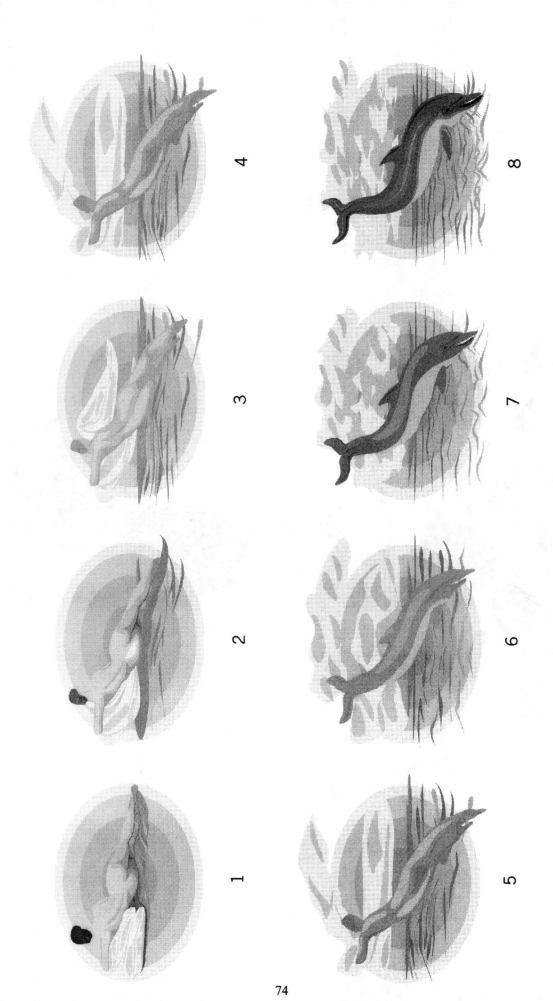

1 2 3 4

5 6 7 8

74

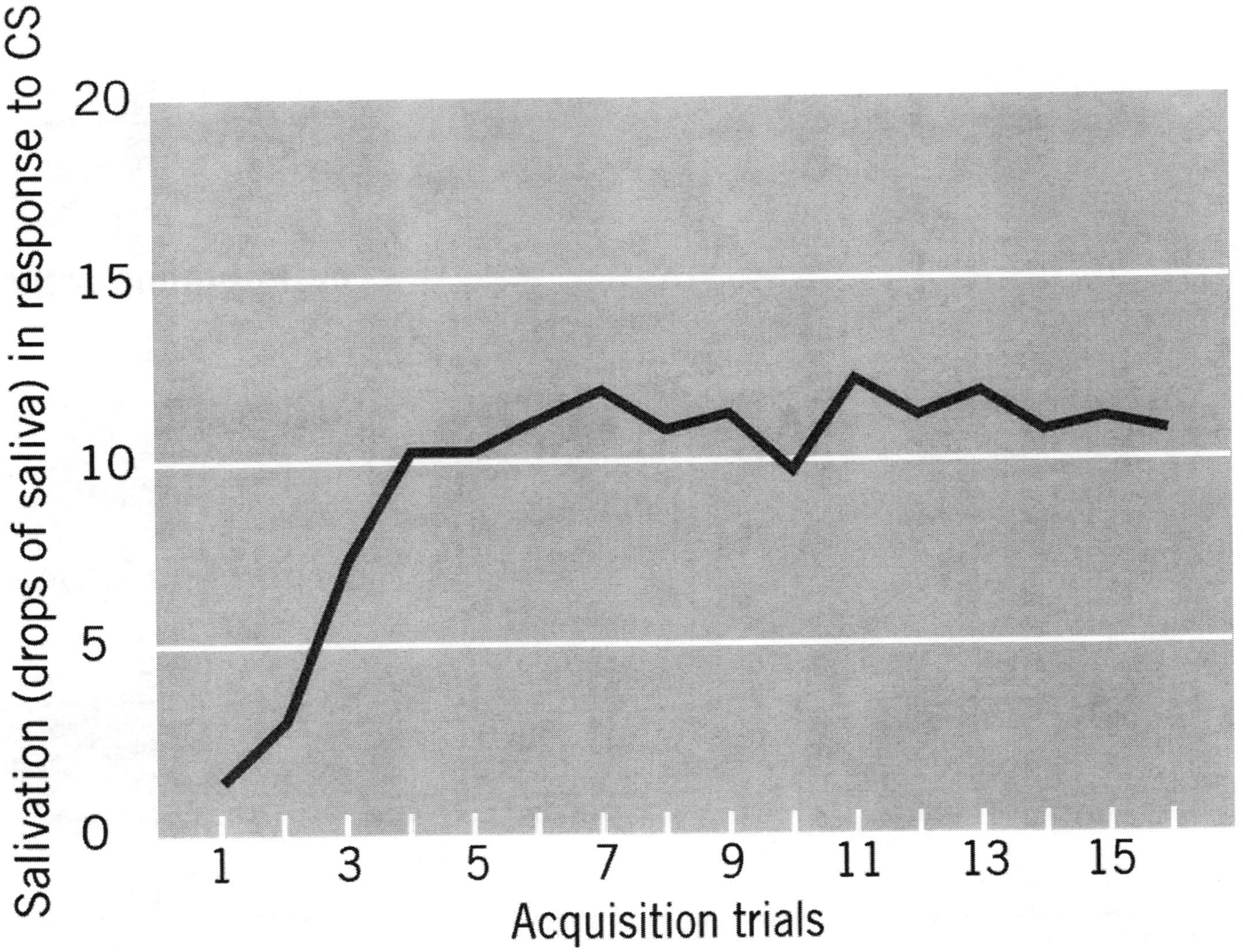
Salivation (drops of saliva) in response to CS
20
15
10
5
0
1
3
5
7
9
11
13
15
Acquisition trials

(Figure adapted from Pavlov, 1927)

© 1999 John Wiley and Sons, Inc.

Westen, 2e Fig. 5.2

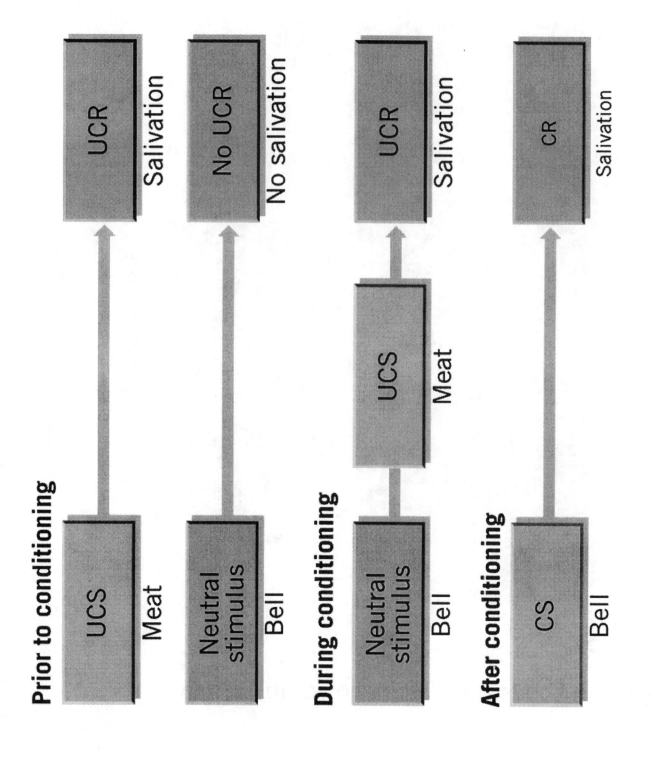

Westen, 2e Fig. 5.3

© 1999 John Wiley and Sons, Inc.

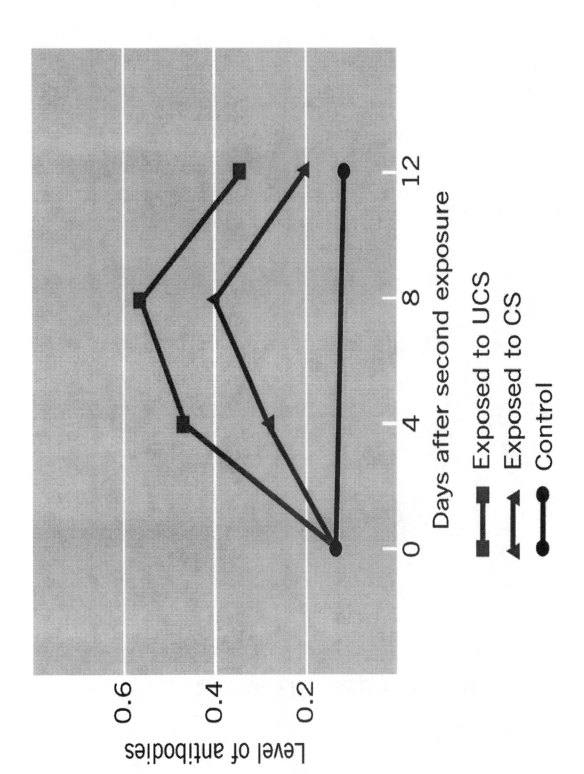

(Figure adapted from Alzarez-Borda et al., 1995)

Westen, 2e Fig. 5.4

Days after second exposure

■ Exposed to UCS
▲ Exposed to CS
● Control

Level of antibodies

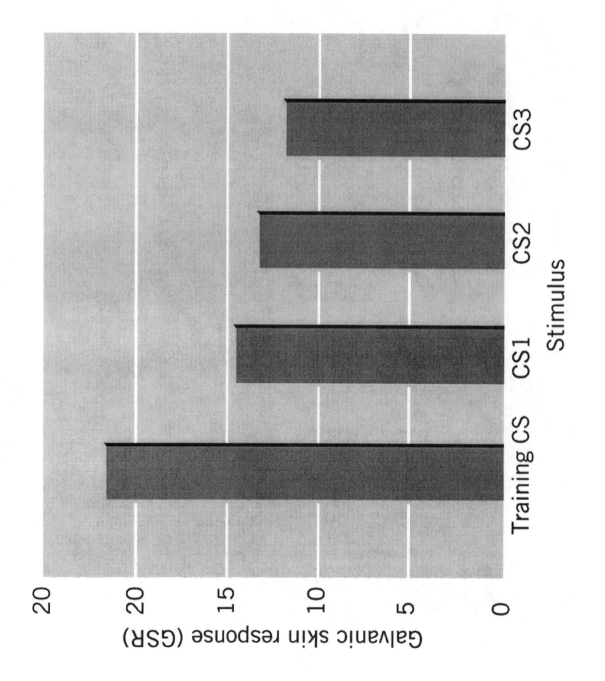

(Figure adapted from Hovland, 1937)

Westen, 2e Fig. 5.5

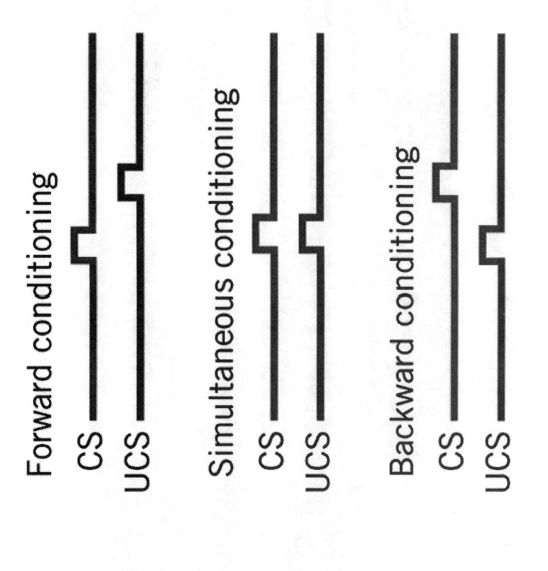

Forward conditioning

CS

UCS

Simultaneous conditioning

CS

UCS

Backward conditioning

CS

UCS

Westen, 2e Fig. 5.6

© 1999 John Wiley and Sons, Inc.

Unconditioned stimulus (ucs)	Conditioned stimulus (cs)		
	Light	Sound	Taste
Shock	Avoidance	Avoidance	No avoidance
X-rays	No avoidance	No avoidance	Avoidance

(Figure adapted from Garcia & Koelling, 1966)

Westen, 2e Fig. 5.7

© 1999 John Wiley and Sons, Inc.

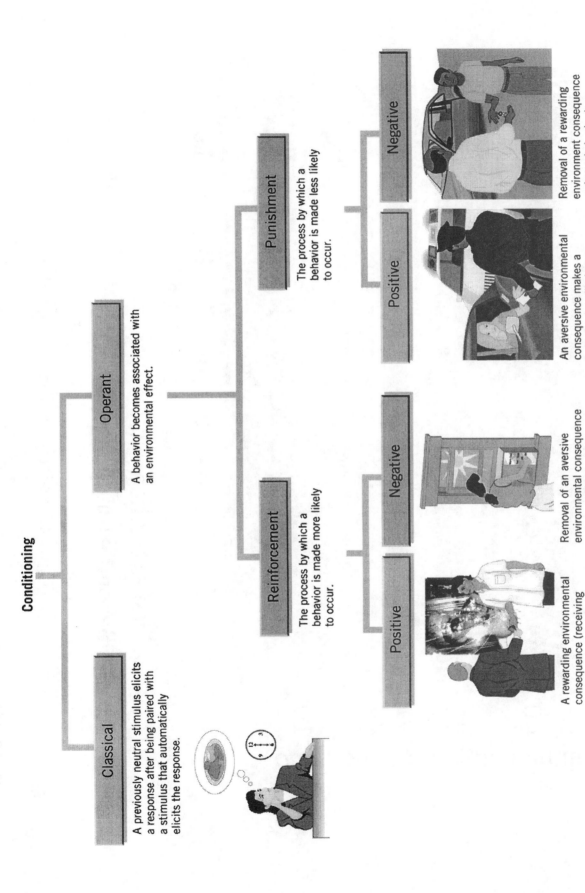

Conditioning

Classical

A previously neutral stimulus elicits a response after being paired with a stimulus that automatically elicits the response.

Operant

A behavior becomes associated with an environmental effect.

Reinforcement

The process by which a behavior is made more likely to occur.

Positive

A rewarding environmental consequence (receiving payment for producing a style of art) makes a behavior more likely to occur.

Negative

Removal of an aversive environmental consequence makes a behavior more likely to occur.

Punishment

The process by which a behavior is made less likely to occur.

Positive

An aversive environmental consequence makes a behavior less likely to occur.

Negative

Removal of a rewarding environment consequence makes a behavior less likely to occur.

Westen, 2e Fig. 5.9

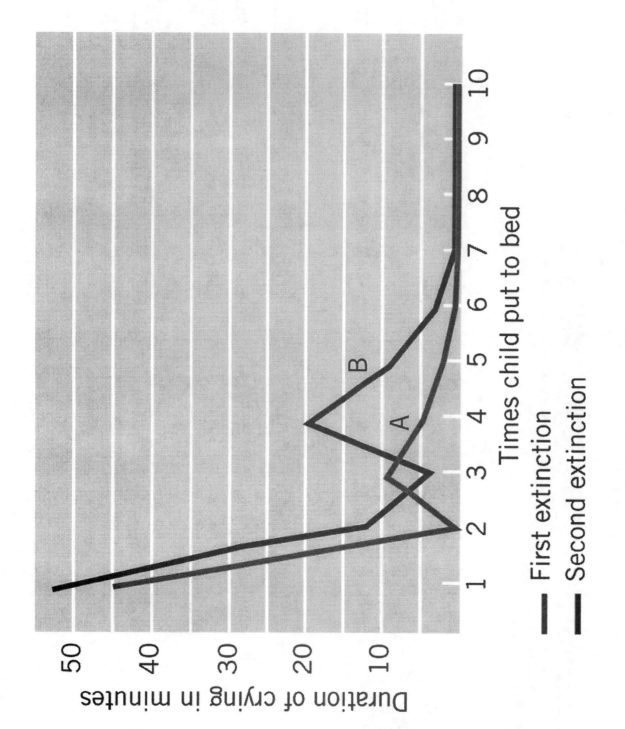

(Figure adapted from Williams, 1959, p. 269)

Westen, 2e Fig. 5.10

© 1999 John Wiley and Sons, Inc.

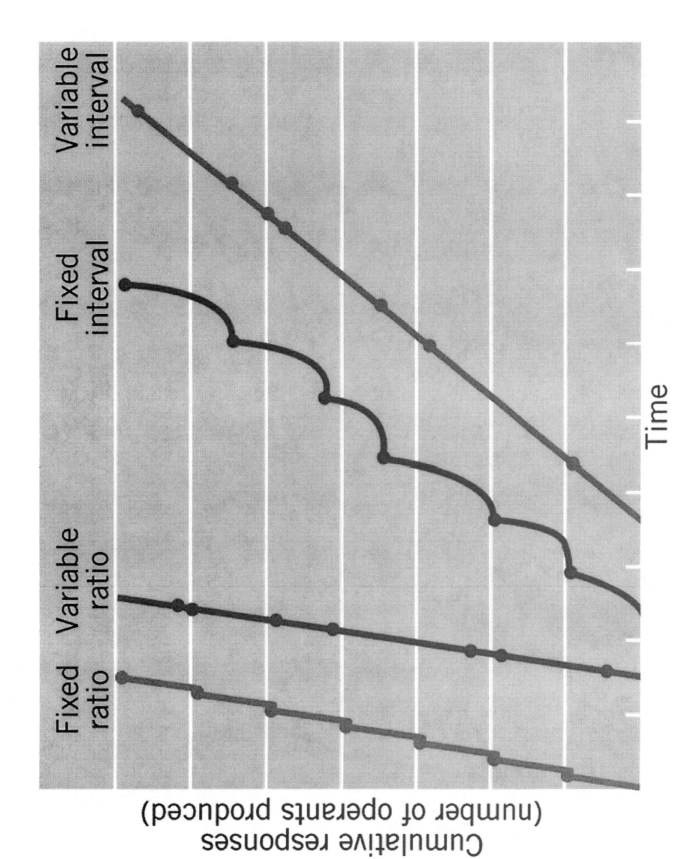

Westen, 2e Fig. 5.11

© 1999 John Wiley and Sons, Inc.

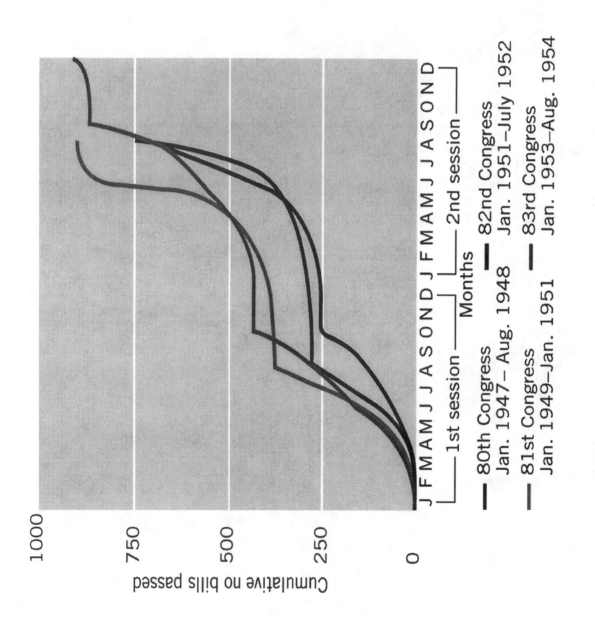

(Figure adapted from Weisberg & Waldrop, 1972, p. 23)

Westen, 2e Fig. 5.12

© 1999 John Wiley and Sons, Inc.

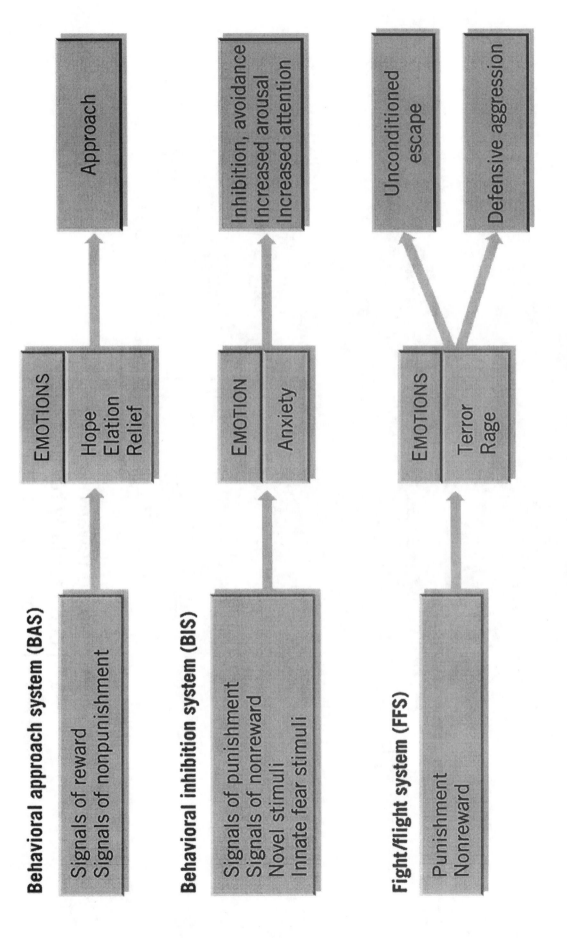

Behavioral approach system (BAS)

Signals of reward
Signals of nonpunishment

EMOTIONS
Hope
Elation
Relief

Approach

Behavioral inhibition system (BIS)

Signals of punishment
Signals of nonreward
Novel stimuli
Innate fear stimuli

EMOTION
Anxiety

Inhibition, avoidance
Increased arousal
Increased attention

Fight/flight system (FFS)

Punishment
Nonreward

EMOTIONS
Terror
Rage

Unconditioned escape

Defensive aggression

(Figure adapted from Gray, 1988, pp. 278-279)

Westen, 2e Fig. 5.13

© 1999 John Wiley and Sons, Inc.

Average errors

Days

— No food reward
— Food regularly rewarded
— No food reward until day 11

(Figure adapted from Tolman & Honzik, 1930, p. 267)

Westen, 2e Fig. 5.14

© 1999 John Wiley and Sons, Inc.

I more strongly believe that

1. Promotions are earned through hard work and persistence.

OR

Making a lot of money is largely a matter of getting the right breaks.

2. In my experience I have noticed that there is usually a direct connection between how hard I study and the grades I get.

OR

Many times the reactions of teachers seem haphazard to me.

3. I am the master of my fate.

OR

A great deal that happens to me is probably a matter of chance.

(Figure adapted from Rotter, 1971)

Westen, 2e Fig. 5.15

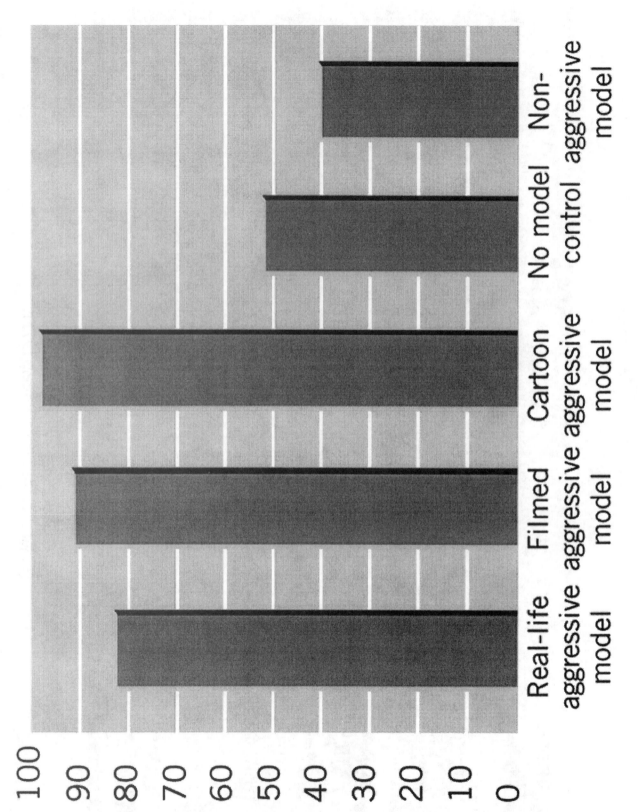

Mean number of aggressive responses

Real-life aggressive model / Filmed aggressive model / Cartoon aggressive model / No model control / Non-aggressive model

© 1999 John Wiley and Sons, Inc.

Westen, 2e Fig. 5.16

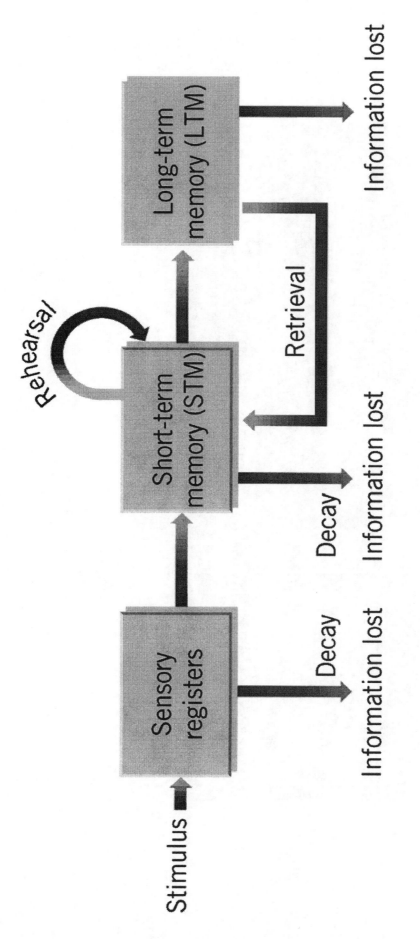

Westen, 2e Fig. 6.01

© 1999 John Wiley and Sons, Inc.

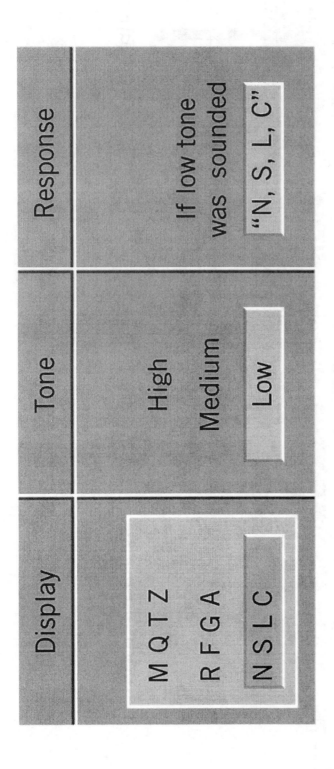

Display	Tone	Response
M Q T Z R F G A N S L C	High Medium Low	If low tone was sounded "N, S, L, C"

(Figure adapted from Sperling, 1960)

Westen, 2e Fig. 6.02

© 1999 John Wiley and Sons, Inc.

(a) **76388826**

(b) 76388826 (20 seconds later)

(c) **9**1888826 (25 seconds later)

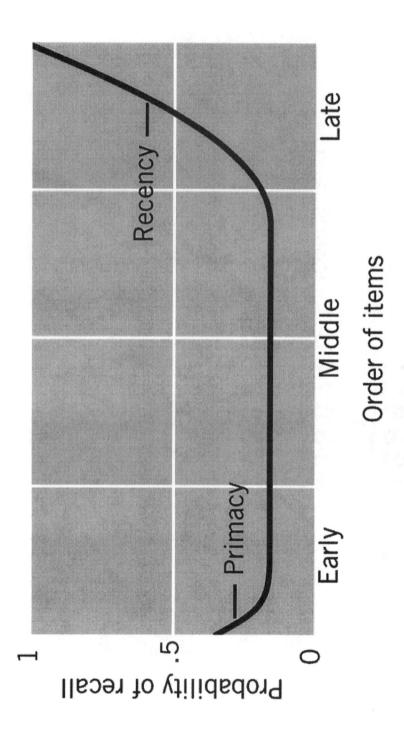

Order of items

Probability of recall

(Figure adapted from Atkinson & Shriffrin, 1968)

Westen, 2e Fig. 6.04

Item presented	Rehearsal
1. Reaction	Reaction, reaction, reaction, reaction
2. Hoof	Hoof, reaction, hoof, reaction
3. Blessing	Blessing, hoof, reaction
4. Research	Research, reaction, hoof, research
5. Candy	Candy, hoof, research, reaction
6. Hardship	Hardship, hoof, hardship, hoof
7. Kindness	Kindness, candy, hardship, hoof
8. Nonsense	Nonsense, kindness, candy, hardships
. . . . .	. . . . .
20. Cellar	Cellar, alcohol, misery, cellar

(Figure adapted from Rundus, 1971)

Westen, 2e Fig. 6.05

© 1999 John Wiley and Sons, Inc.

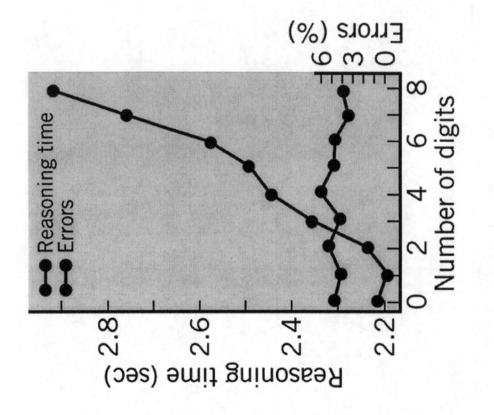

(Figure adapted from Baddeley, 1995)

Westen, 2e Fig. 6.06

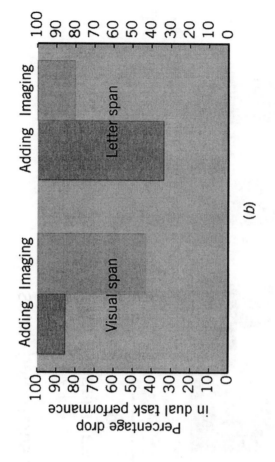

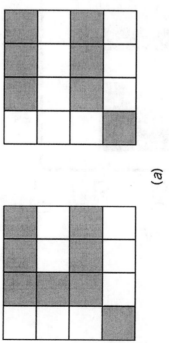

(Figure adapted from Logie, 1996)

Westen, 2e Fig. 6.07a,b

© 1999 John Wiley and Sons, Inc.

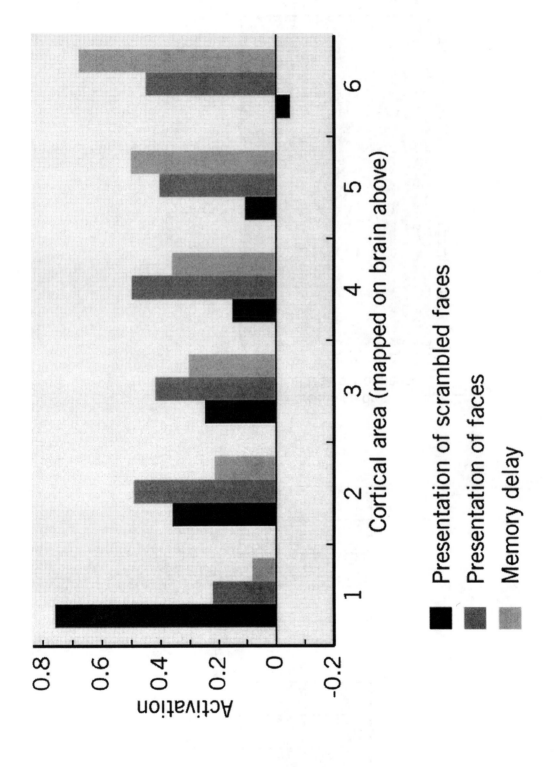

Cortical area (mapped on brain above)

Activation

■ Presentation of scrambled faces
■ Presentation of faces
■ Memory delay

(b)

(Figure adapted from Courtney et al., 1997)

Westen, 2e Fig. 6.08

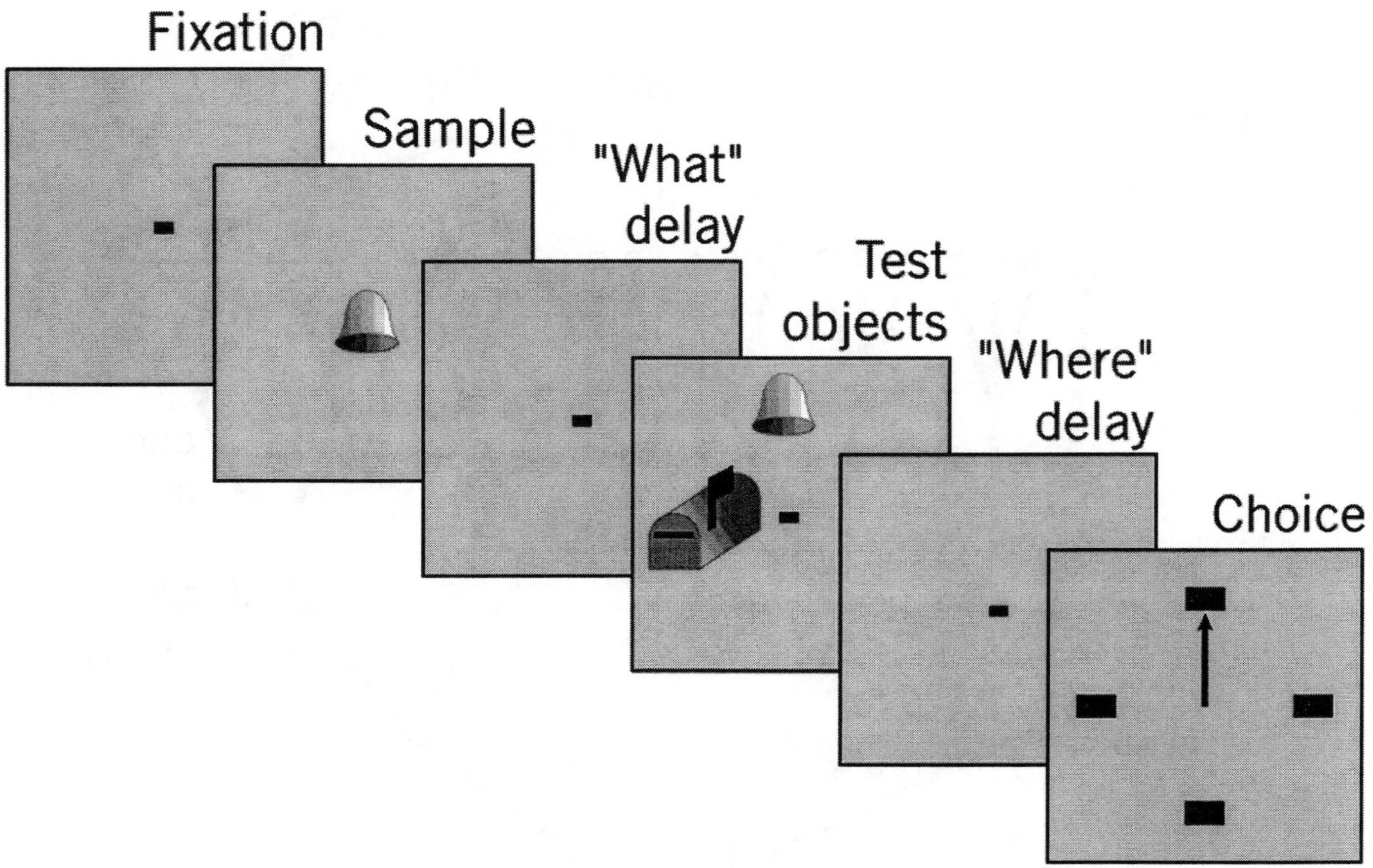

Fixation Sample "What" delay Test objects "Where" delay Choice

(Figure adapted from Rao et al., 1997)

Westen, 2e Fig. 6.09

© 1999 John Wiley and Sons, Inc.

97

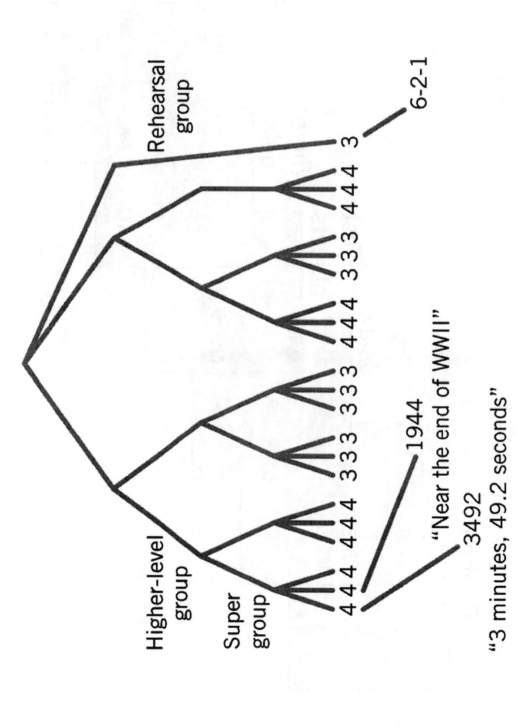

(Figure adapted from Ericsson & Chase, 1982)

Westen, 2e Fig. 6.10

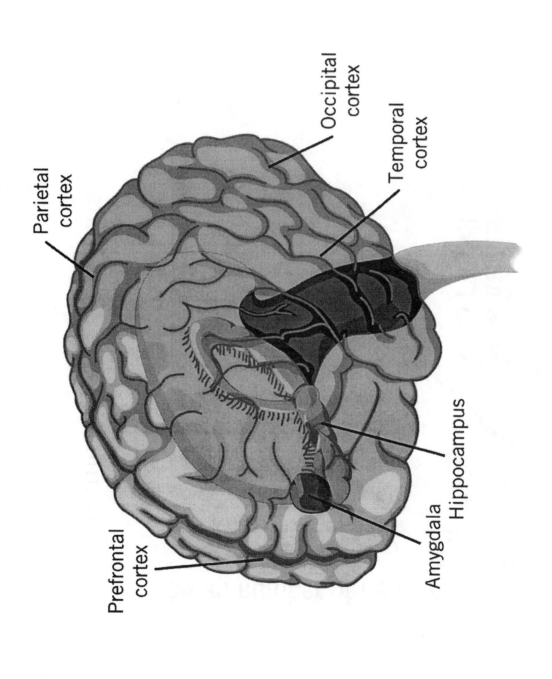

Parietal
cortex

Occipital
cortex

Temporal
cortex

Prefrontal
cortex

Amygdala

Hippocampus

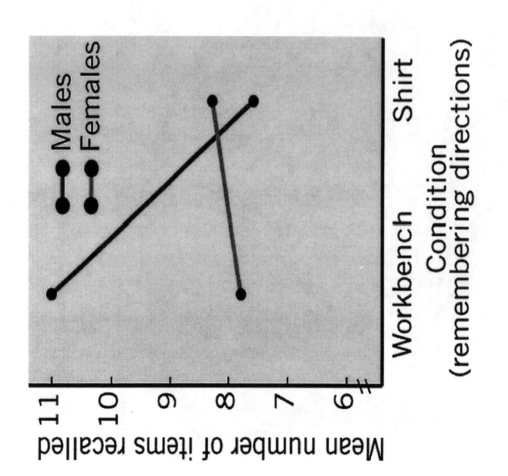

Figure adapted from Herrmann et al., 1992)

Westen, 2e Fig. 6.12

© 1999 John Wiley and Sons, Inc.

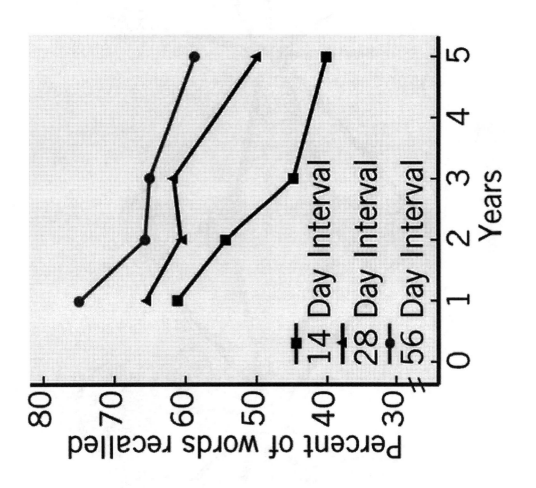

(Figure adapted from Bahrick et al., 1993)

Westen, 2e Fig. 6.14

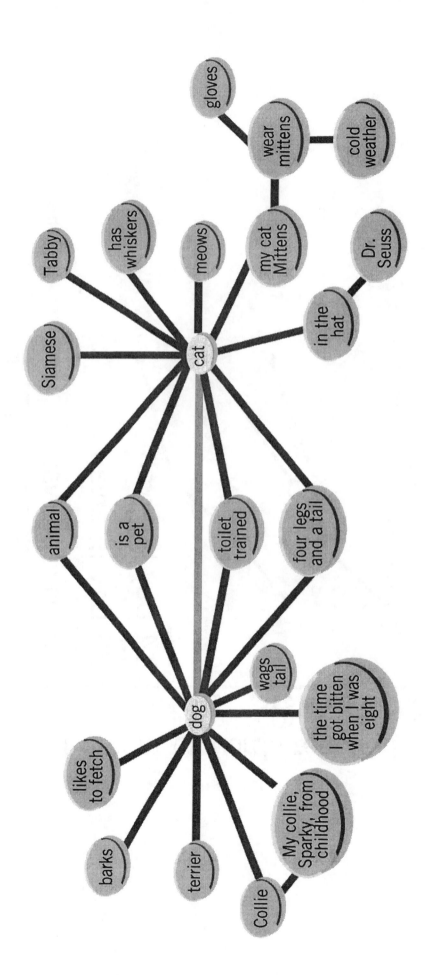

Westen, 2e Fig. 6.15

© 1999 John Wiley and Sons, Inc.

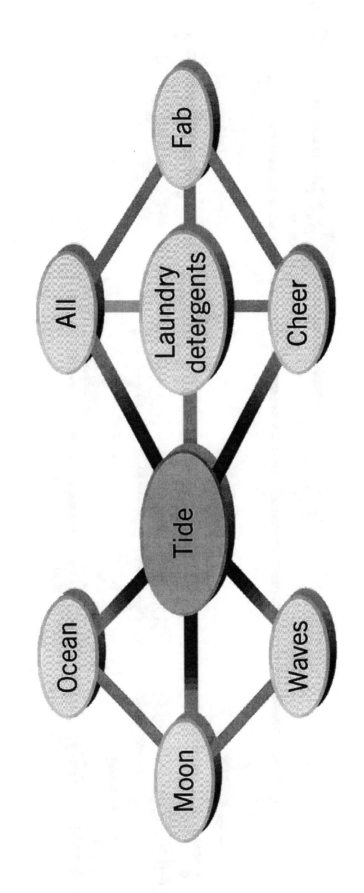

Westen, 2e Fig. 6.16

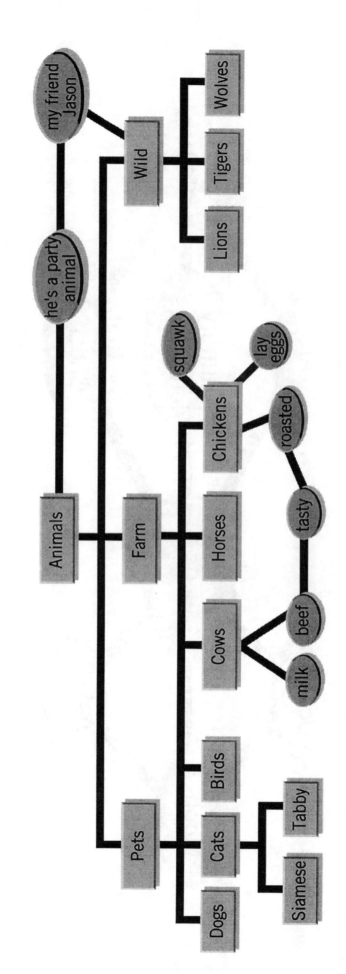

Westen, 2e Fig. 6.17

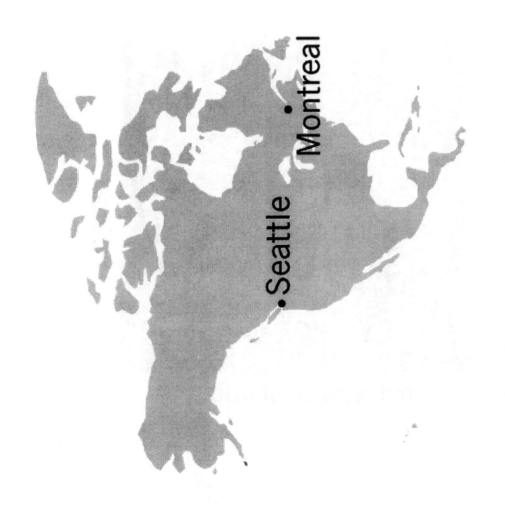

Seattle

Montreal

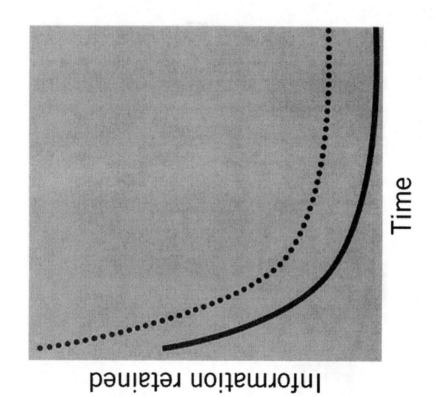

Time

Information retained

(Figure adapted from Bahrick et al., 1996)

Westen, 2e Fig. 6.20

© 1999 John Wiley and Sons, Inc.

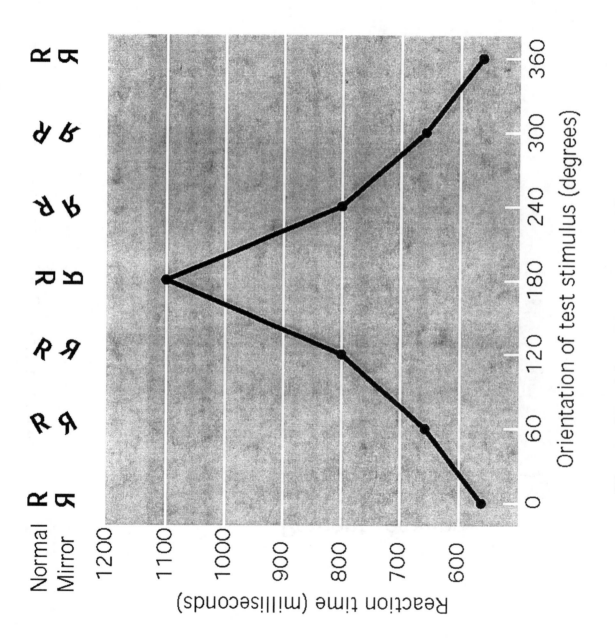

Orientation of test stimulus (degrees)

Reaction time (milliseconds)

Normal R Я R Я R Я Я R
Mirror Я Я Я Я Я Я

(Figure adapted from Cooper & Shepherd, 1973)

Westen, 2e Fig. 7.01

© 1999 John Wiley and Sons, Inc.

SHAPE

DEFINING
FEATURES

- electronic device
- has a particular architecture, or operating design
- uses digital processor to perform computations

CHARACTERISTIC
FEATURES

- has a keyboard
- has a screen
- can be used for word processing
- can store information on hard drive or disks

EXEMPLARS

- IBM Pentium
- Macintosh

Westen, 2e Fig. 7.02

© 1999 John Wiley and Sons, Inc.

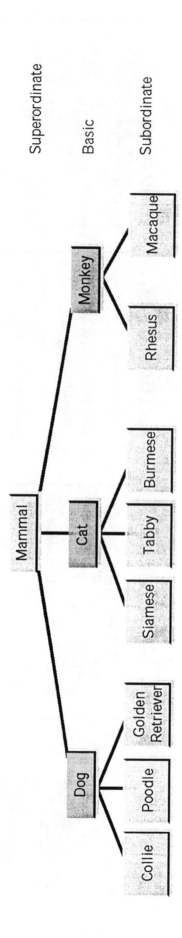

Superordinate

Basic

Subordinate

Mammal

Dog — Collie, Poodle, Golden Retriever

Cat — Siamese, Tabby, Burmese

Monkey — Rhesus, Macaque

Westen, 2e Fig. 7.03

© 1999 John Wiley and Sons, Inc.

110

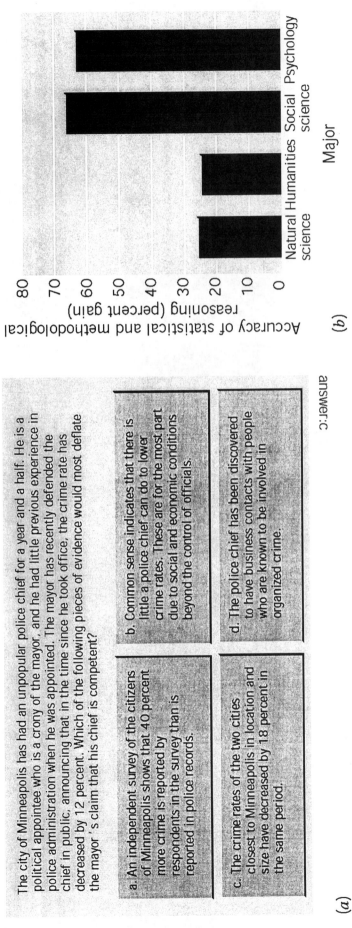

The city of Minneapolis has had an unpopular police chief for a year and a half. He is a political appointee who is a crony of the mayor, and he had little previous experience in police administration when he was appointed. The mayor has recently defended the chief in public, announcing that in the time since he took office, the crime rate has decreased by 12 percent. Which of the following pieces of evidence would most deflate the mayor's claim that his chief is competent?

a. An independent survey of the citizens of Minneapolis shows that 40 percent more crime is reported by respondents in the survey than is reported in police records.

b. Common sense indicates that there is little a police chief can do to lower crime rates. These are for the most part due to social and economic conditions beyond the control of officials.

c. The crime rates of the two cities closest to Minneapolis in location and size have decreased by 18 percent in the same period.

d. The police chief has been discovered to have business contacts with people who are known to be involved in organized crime.

answer: c

(a)

(b)

(Figures adapted from Lehman et al., 1988; Lehman & Nisbett, 1990)

Westen, 2e Fig. 7.04

© 1999 John Wiley and Sons, Inc.

111

(Figure adapted from Wason, 1968)

Westen, 2e Fig. 7.05

In a crackdown against drunk drivers, Massachusetts law enforcement officials are revoking liquor licenses left and right. You are a bouncer in a Boston bar, and you'll lose your job unless you enforce the following law:

If a person is drinking beer, then he or she must be at least 21 years old.

In front of you are four cards belonging to four patrons of your bar. Each card has the person's age on one side and what she or he is drinking on the other. Which cards must you turn over to ensure that the law is being followed?

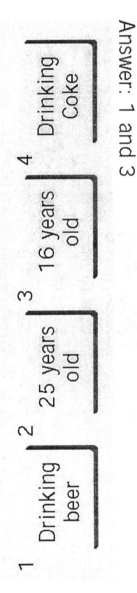

| 1 Drinking beer | 2 25 years old | 3 16 years old | 4 Drinking Coke |

Answer: 1 and 3

(Figure adapted from Griggs & Cox, 1982)

Westen, 2e Fig. 7.06

Initial state

A problem

Operators

Actions performed
to solve the problem

Goal
state

No problem

The problem space

Westen, 2e Fig. 7.07

© 1999 John Wiley and Sons, Inc.

114

CONDITION

Outcome	Mental simulation	Positive thinking	Control
Number of hours studying	16.07	11.57	14.50
Grade (% of questions correct)	80.60	72.57	77.68

Westen, 2e Fig. 7.08

(Figure adapted from Rumelhart, 1984, p.8)

Westen, 2e Fig. 7.10

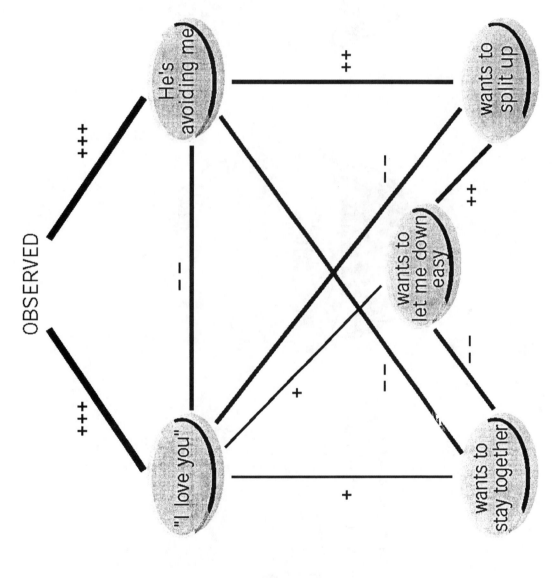

OBSERVED

He's avoiding me

wants to split up

"I love you"

wants to let me down easy

wants to stay together

+++

+++

++

+

+

+

++

−

−

−

−

−

Westen, 2e Fig. 7.11

© 1999 John Wiley and Sons, Inc.

117

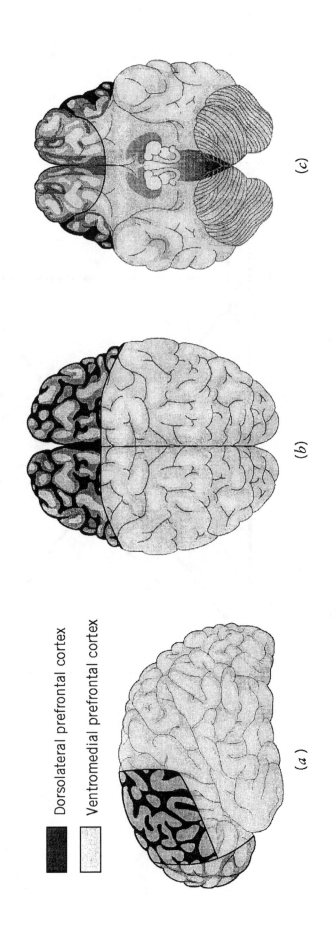

Dorsolateral prefrontal cortex

Ventromedial prefrontal cortex

(a)

(b)

(c)

Westen, 2e Fig. 7.12

© 1999 John Wiley and Sons, Inc.

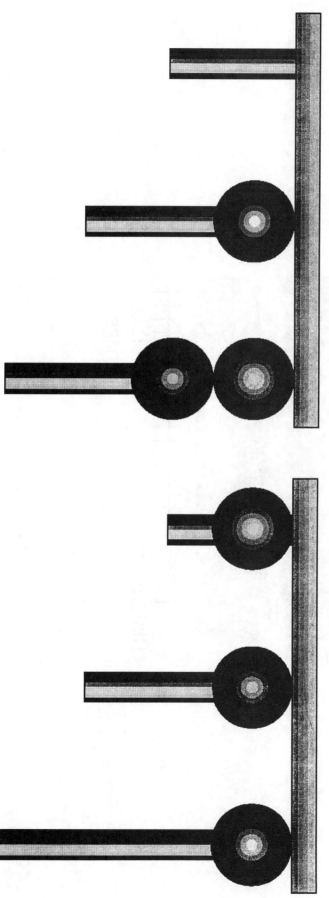

(Figure adapted from Frith & Dolan, 1996)

Westen, 2e Fig. 7.13

© 1999 John Wiley and Sons, Inc.

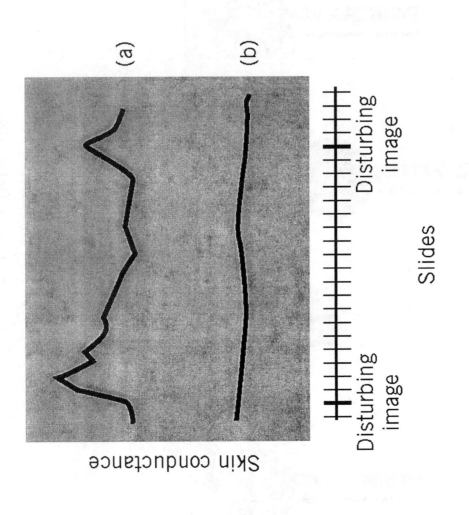

(Figure adapted from Damasio, 1994)

Westen, 2e Fig. 7.14

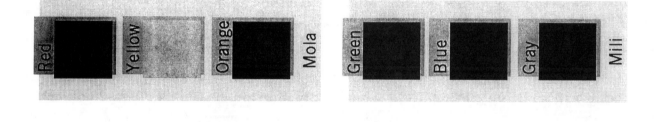

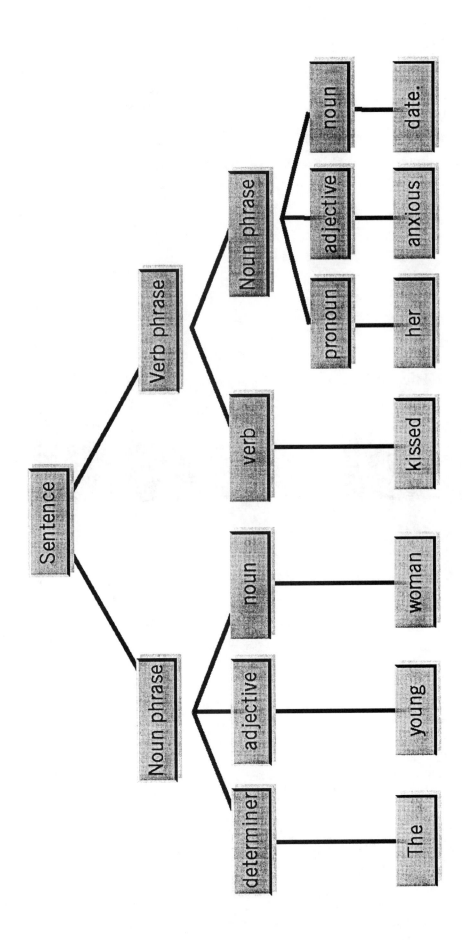

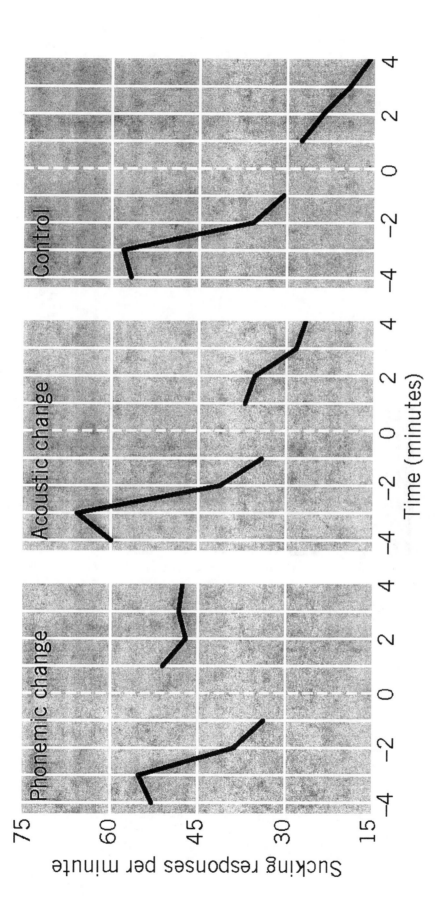

(Figure adapted from Eimas, 1985)

Westen, 2e Fig. 7.17

© 1999 John Wiley and Sons, Inc.

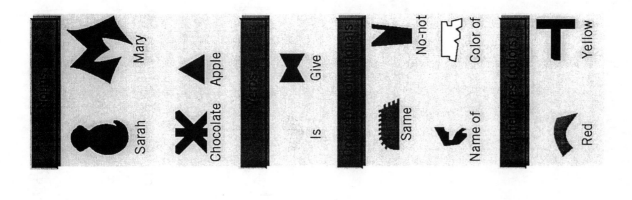

(Figure adapted from Premack & Premack, 1972)

Westen, 2e Fig. 7.18

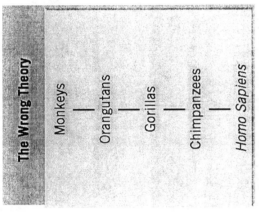

The Wrong Theory

Monkeys
Orangutans
Gorillas
Chimpanzees
Homo Sapiens

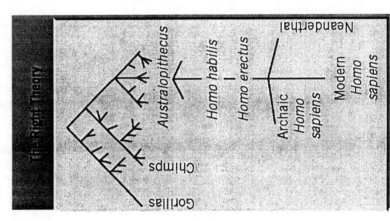

The Right Theory

Gorillas
Chimps
Australopithecus
Homo habilis
Homo erectus
Archaic *Homo sapiens*
Neanderthal
Modern *Homo sapiens*

(Figure adapted from Pinker, 1994)

Westen, 2e Fig. 7.20

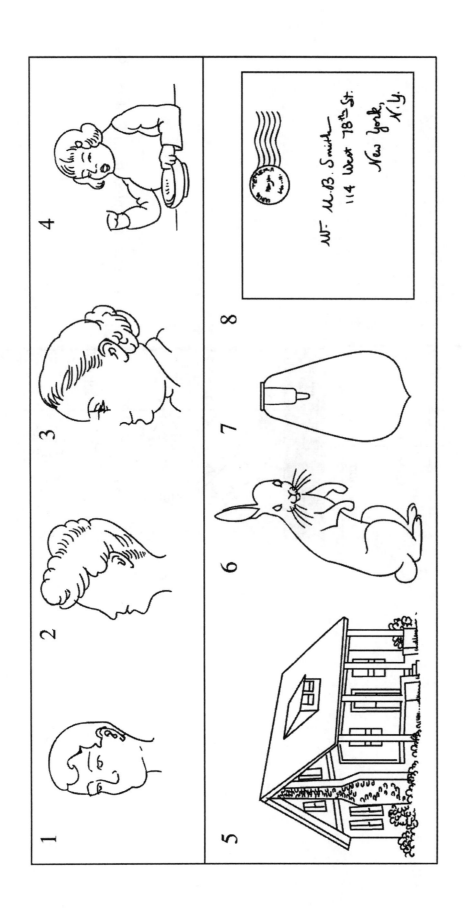

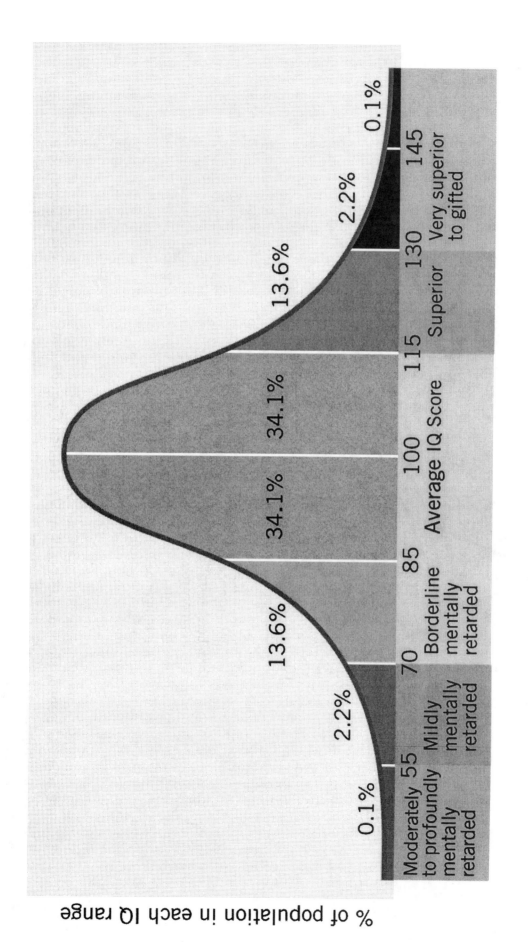

% of population in each IQ range

55 Moderately to profoundly mentally retarded
Mildly mentally retarded
70 Borderline mentally retarded
85 Average IQ Score
100
115 Superior
130 Very superior to gifted
145

0.1%
2.2%
13.6%
34.1%
34.1%
13.6%
2.2%
0.1%

(Figure adapted from Anastasi & Urbina, 1997)

Westen, 2e Fig. 8.02

© 1999 John Wiley and Sons, Inc.

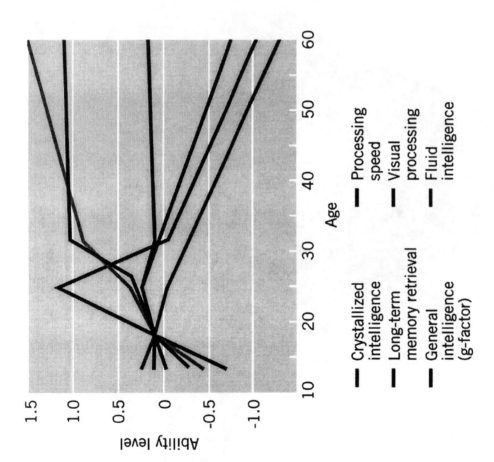

(Figure adapted from J. Horn & J. Knoll (1997) Human Cognitive Abilities: Gf-Gc theory. In D.P. Flanagan, J.L. Gershaft, & P.L. Harrison (Eds). Contemporary Intellectual Assessment, New York: Guilford, p. 72)

Westen, 2e Fig. 8.03

© 1999 John Wiley and Sons, Inc.

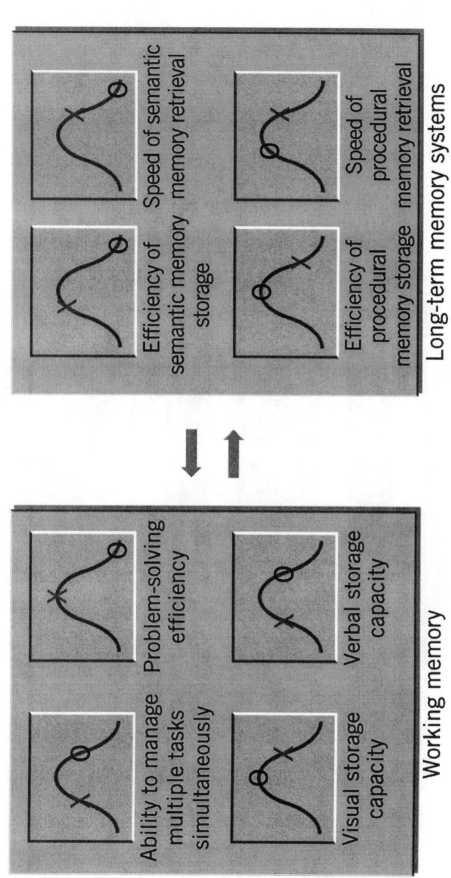

Long-term memory systems

Working memory

X = subject 1
O = subject 2

Speed of semantic memory retrieval

Efficiency of semantic memory storage

Speed of procedural memory retrieval

Efficiency of procedural memory storage

Problem-solving efficiency

Ability to manage multiple tasks simultaneously

Verbal storage capacity

Visual storage capacity

Westen, 2e Fig. 8.04

© 1999 John Wiley and Sons, Inc.

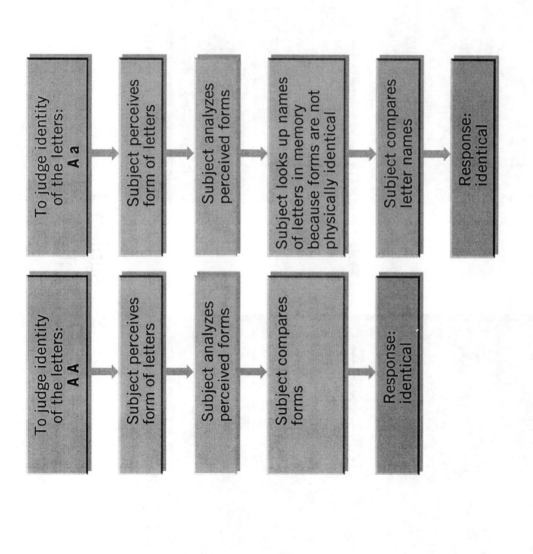

(Figure adapted from Posner et al., 1969)

Westen, 2e Fig. 8.05

© 1999 John Wiley and Sons, Inc.

(Figure adapted from Mumaw & Pellegrino, 1984)

Westen, 2e Fig. 8.06

© 1999 John Wiley and Sons, Inc.

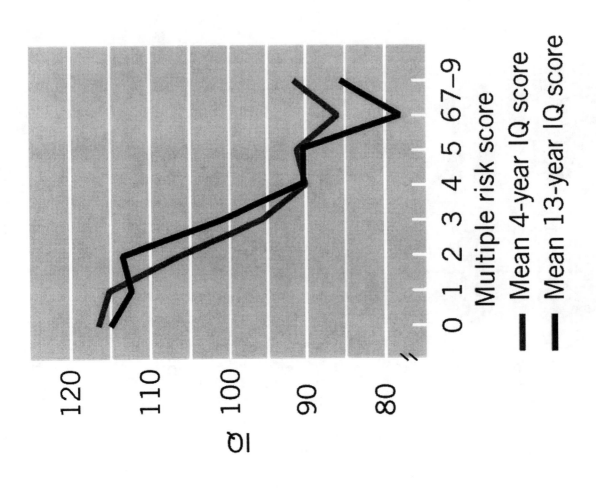

IQ

120

110

100

90

80

0 1 2 3 4 5 6 7–9

Multiple risk score

—— Mean 4-year IQ score

—— Mean 13-year IQ score

(Figure adapted from Sameroff et al., 1993, p. 89)

Westen, 2e Fig. 8.07

© 1999 John Wiley and Sons, Inc.

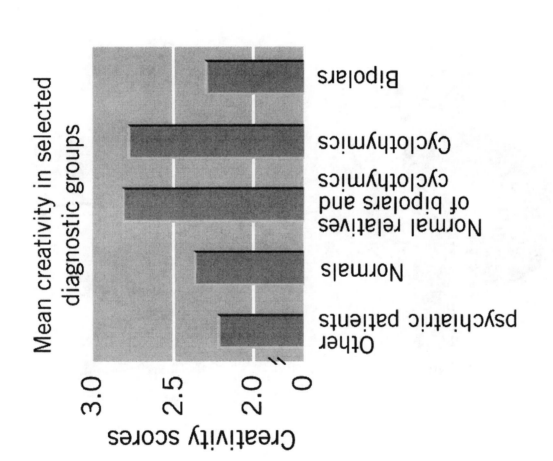

Mean creativity in selected diagnostic groups

Creativity scores

3.0 — 2.5 — 2.0 — 1 — 0

Bipolars

Cyclothymics

Normal relatives of bipolars and cyclothymics

Normals

Other psychiatric patients

(Figure adapted from Richards et al., 1988, p. 286)

Westen, 2e Fig. 8.08

© 1999 John Wiley and Sons, Inc.

133

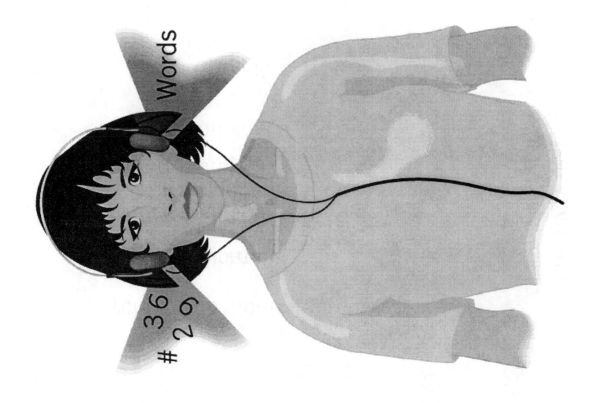

Words

#36
#26

Westen, 2e Fig. 9.01

© 1999 John Wiley and Sons, Inc.

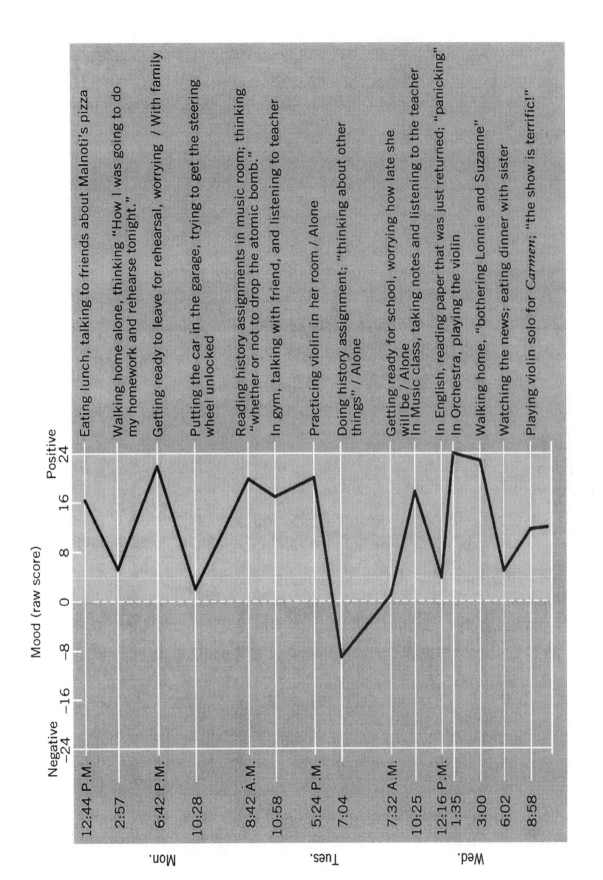

(Figure adapted from Csikszentmihalyi & Larson, 1984, p. 117)

Westen, 2e Fig. 9.02

© 1999 John Wiley and Sons, Inc.

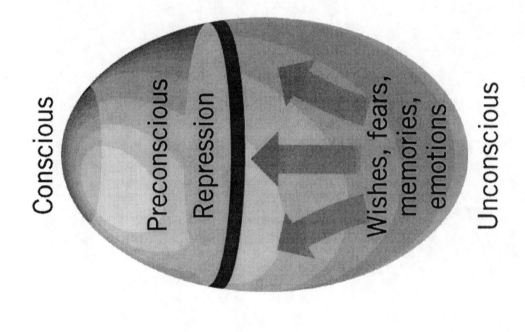

Conscious

Preconscious

Repression

Wishes, fears, memories, emotions

Unconscious

Westen, 2e Fig. 9.03

© 1999 John Wiley and Sons, Inc.

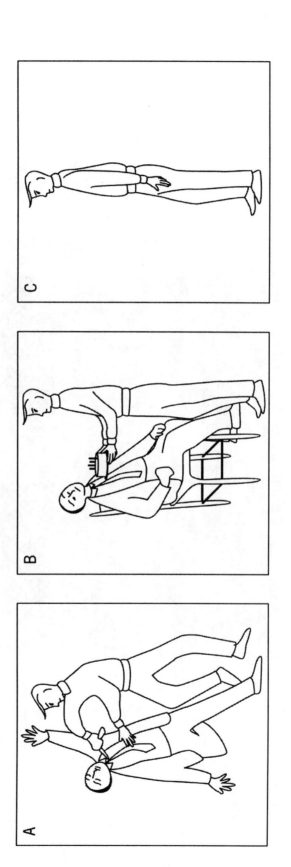

(Figure adapted from Eagle, 1959)

Westen, 2e Fig. 9.04

© 1999 John Wiley and Sons, Inc.

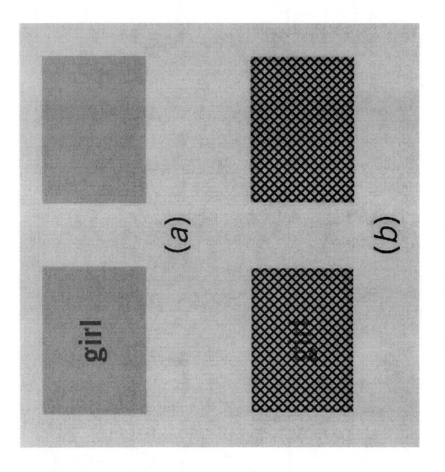

(Figure adapted from Marcel, 1983)

© 1999 John Wiley and Sons, Inc.

Westen, 2e Fig. 9.05

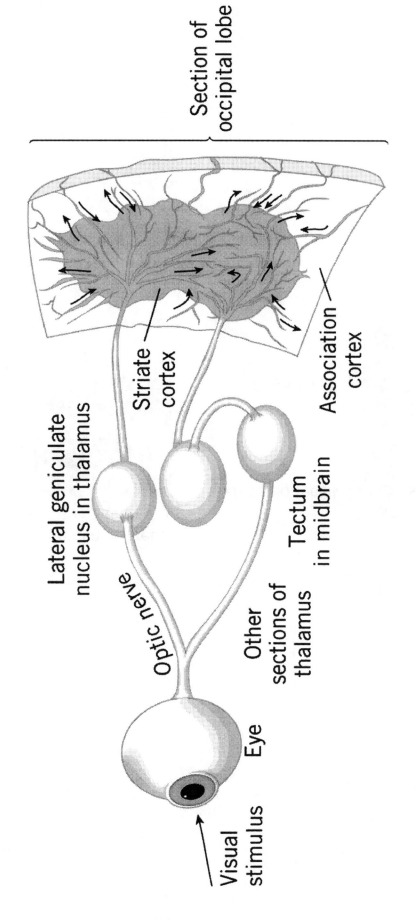

Visual stimulus

Eye

Optic nerve

Lateral geniculate nucleus in thalamus

Other sections of thalamus

Tectum in midbrain

Striate cortex

Association cortex

Section of occipital lobe

Westen, 2e Fig. 9.06

© 1999 John Wiley and Sons, Inc.

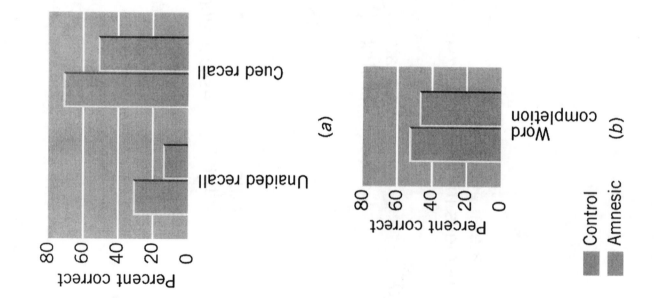

(Figure adapted from Squire, 1986)

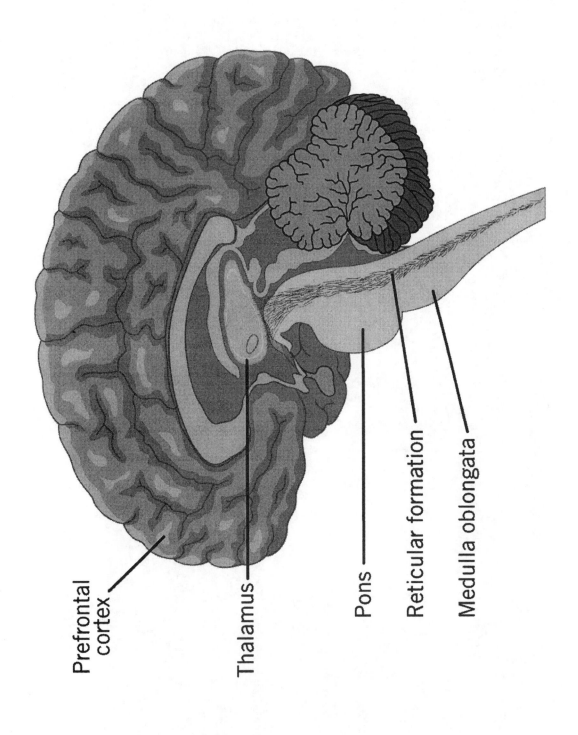

Prefrontal cortex

Thalamus

Pons

Reticular formation

Medulla oblongata

Westen, 2e Fig. 9.08

© 1999 John Wiley and Sons, Inc.

Horse   Sheep   Human   Gorilla   Cat   Opossum

Average sleep (hours)

20 18 16 14 12 10 8 6 4 2 0

Westen, 2e Fig. 9.09

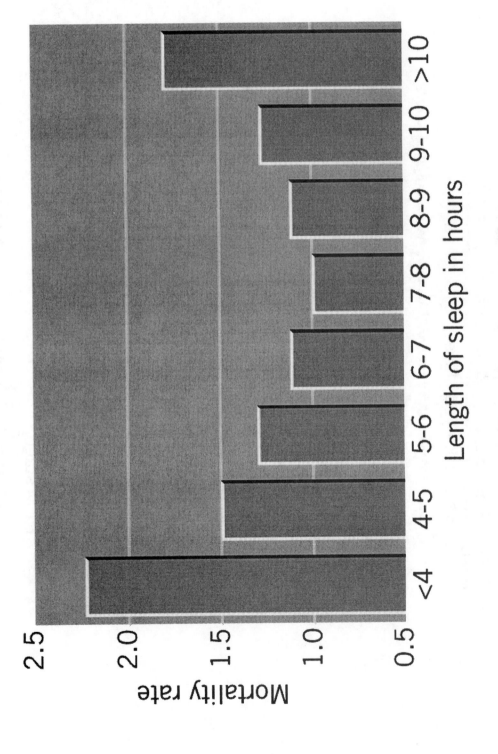

Length of sleep in hours

Mortality rate

(Figure adapted from Kripke et al., 1979)

Westen, 2e Fig. 9.10

© 1999 John Wiley and Sons, Inc.

Awake

Alert

(Beta waves)

Relaxed, eyes closed

(Alpha waves)

NREM Sleep

Stage 1

(Theta waves)

Stage 2

K-complex

Spindles

Stage 3

Delta waves

(Delta waves appear)

Stage 4

(Mostly Delta waves)

REM Sleep

REM stage

(Resembles waking activity)

Westen, 2e Fig. 9.11

© 1999 John Wiley and Sons, Inc.

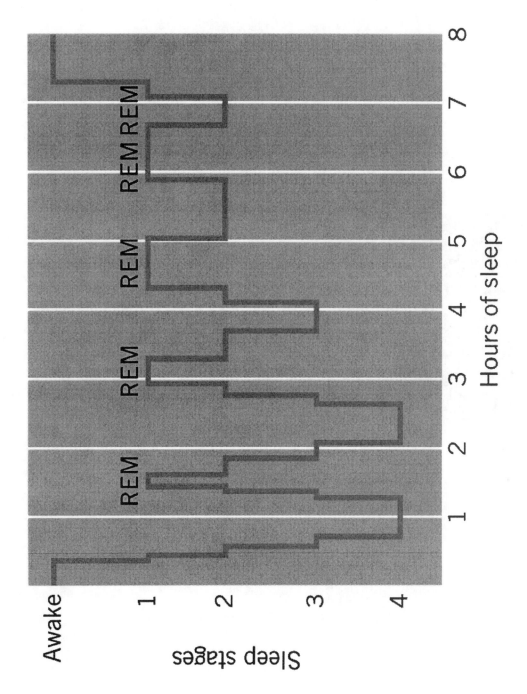

(Figure adapted from Cartwright, 1978)

Westen, 2e Fig. 9.12

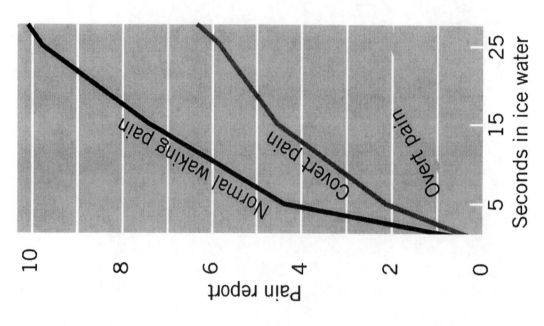

(Figure adapted from Hilgard, 1986, p. 190)

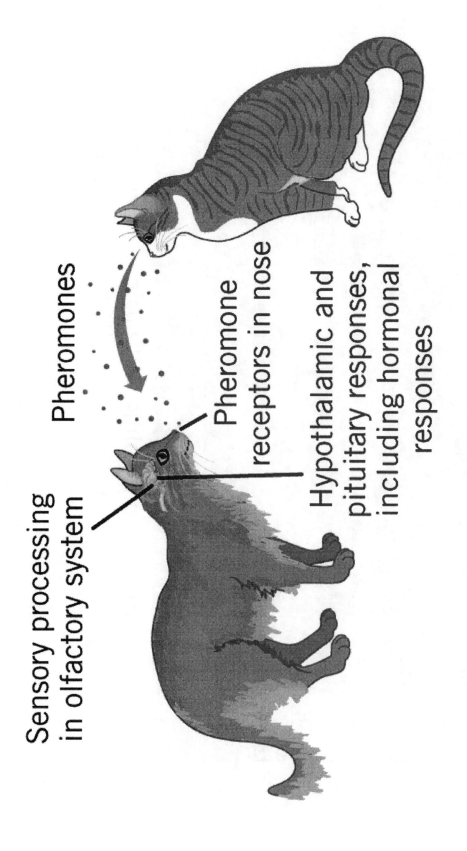

Pheromones

Sensory processing in olfactory system

Pheromone receptors in nose

Hypothalamic and pituitary responses, including hormonal responses

Westen, 2e Fig. 10.01

© 1999 John Wiley and Sons, Inc.

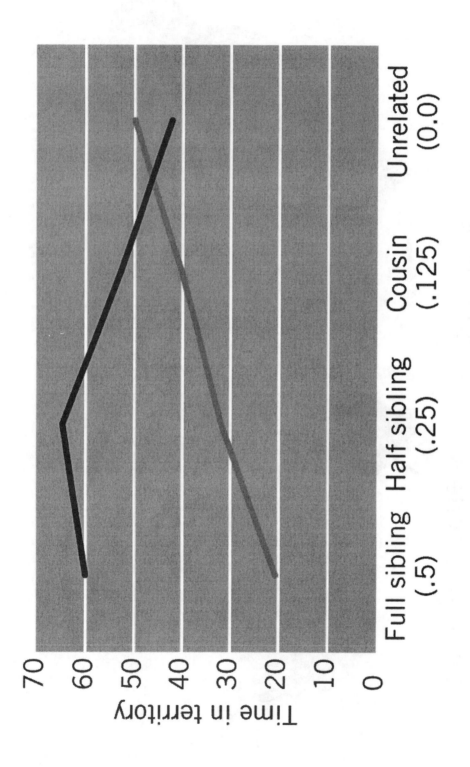

(Figure adapted from Simmons, 1990, p. 194)

Westen, 2e Fig. 10.02

© 1999 John Wiley and Sons, Inc.

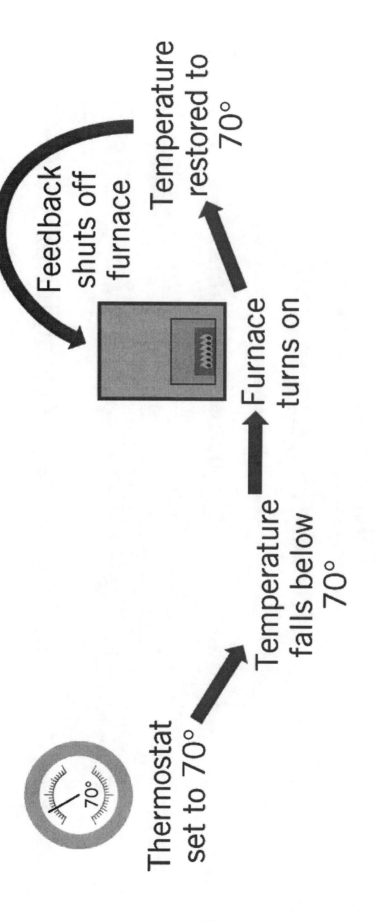

Thermostat set to 70°

Temperature falls below 70°

Furnace turns on

Feedback shuts off furnace

Temperature restored to 70°

Westen, 2e Fig. 10.03

© 1999 John Wiley and Sons, Inc.

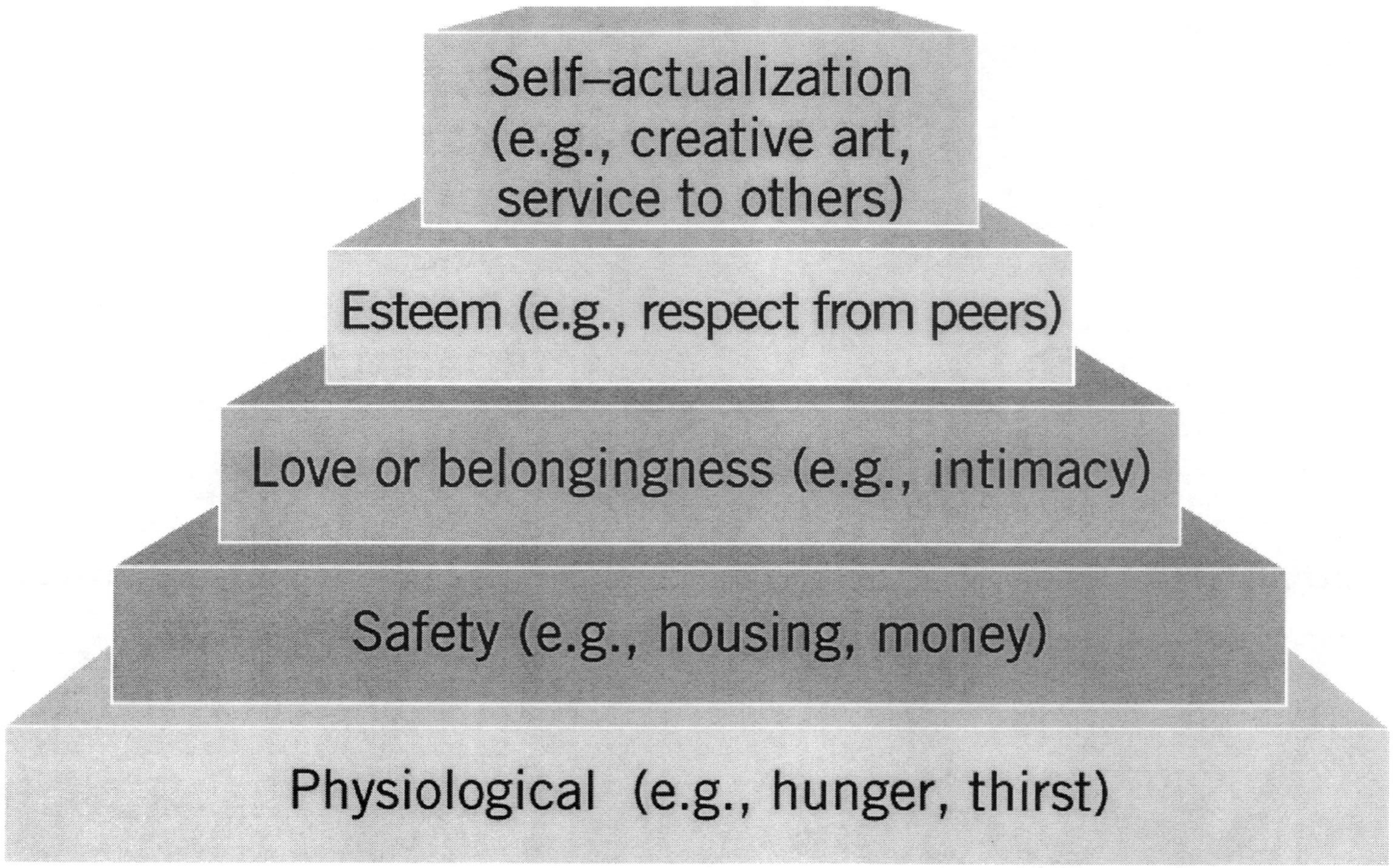

Self-actualization (e.g., creative art, service to others)

Esteem (e.g., respect from peers)

Love or belongingness (e.g., intimacy)

Safety (e.g., housing, money)

Physiological (e.g., hunger, thirst)

Westen, 2e Fig. 10.04

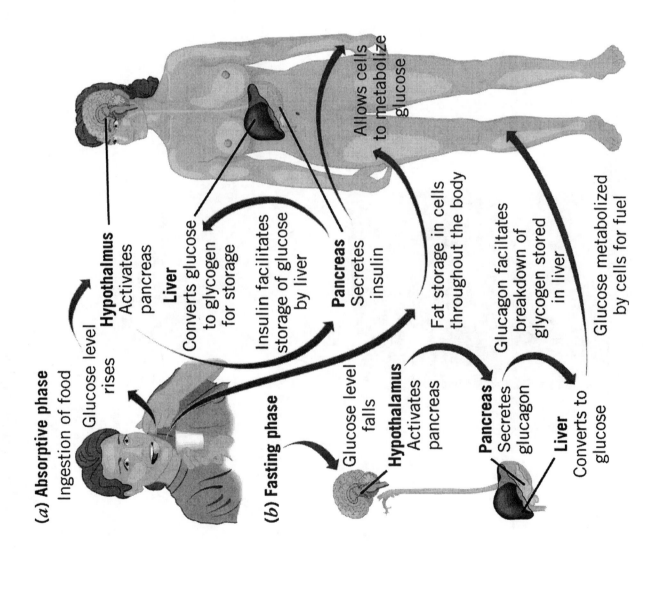

(a) **Absorptive phase**
Ingestion of food

Glucose level rises

Hypothalmus
Activates pancreas

Liver
Converts glucose to glycogen for storage

Insulin facilitates storage of glucose by liver

Pancreas
Secretes insulin

Allows cells to metabolize glucose

Fat storage in cells throughout the body

(b) **Fasting phase**

Glucose level falls

Hypothalamus
Activates pancreas

Pancreas
Secretes glucagon

Liver
Converts to glucose

Glucagon faciltates breakdown of glycogen stored in liver

Glucose metabolized by cells for fuel

Westen, 2e Fig. 10.05

© 1999 John Wiley and Sons, Inc.

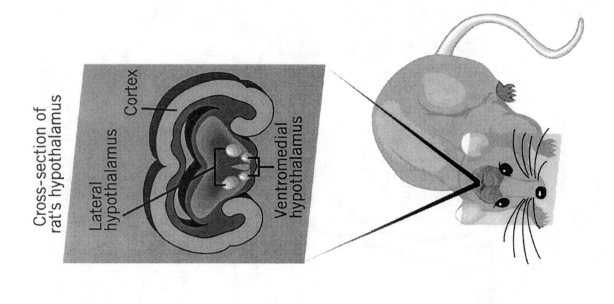

Cross-section of rat's hypothalamus

Cortex

Lateral hypothalamus

Ventromedial hypothalamus

Westen, 2e Fig. 10.06

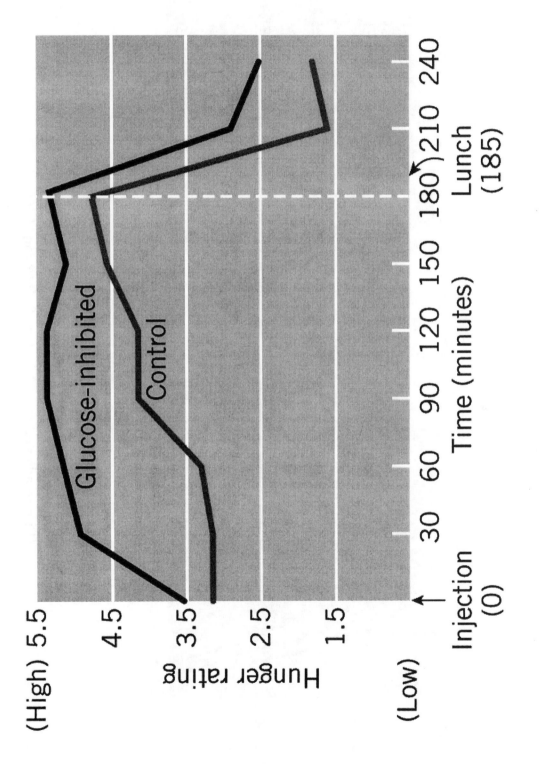

(Figure adapted from Thompson & Campbell, 1977)

Westen, 2e Fig. 10.07

© 1999 John Wiley and Sons, Inc.

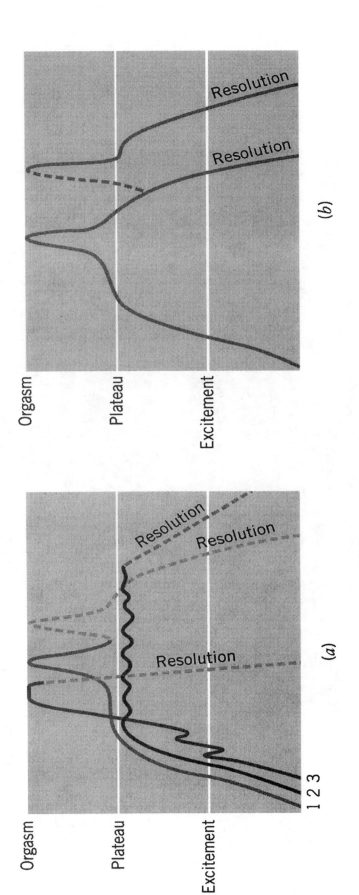

(Figure adapted from Masters & Johnson, 1966)

Westen, 2e Fig. 10.08

© 1999 John Wiley and Sons, Inc.

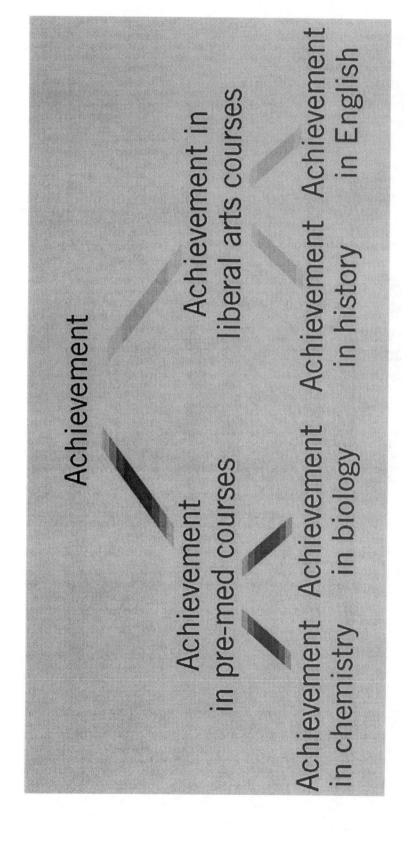

Achievement

Achievement in pre-med courses

Achievement in liberal arts courses

Achievement in chemistry

Achievement in biology

Achievement in history

Achievement in English

Westen, 2e Fig. 10.10

(Figure adapted from A.J. Elliot & M.A. Church (1977), A hierarchical model of approach and avoidance achievement motivation. J. Personality & Social Psych., 72, 218-232, p 227)

Westen, 2e Fig. 10.11

© 1999 John Wiley and Sons, Inc.

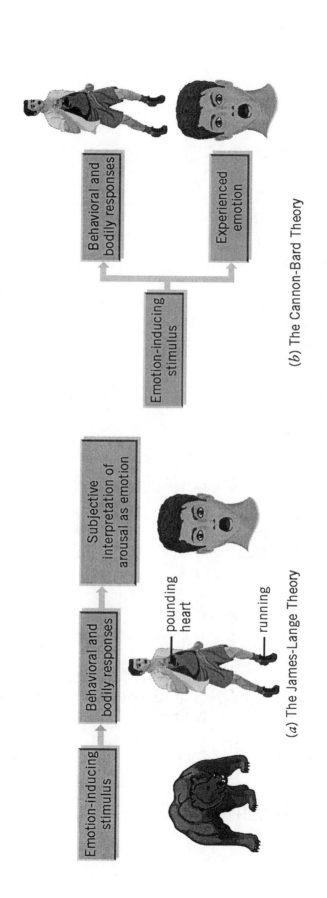

(b) The Cannon-Bard Theory

Behavioral and bodily responses

Experienced emotion

Emotion-inducing stimulus

Subjective interpretation of arousal as emotion

Behavioral and bodily responses

Emotion-inducing stimulus

pounding heart

running

(a) The James-Lange Theory

Westen, 2e Fig. 11.01

© 1999 John Wiley and Sons, Inc.

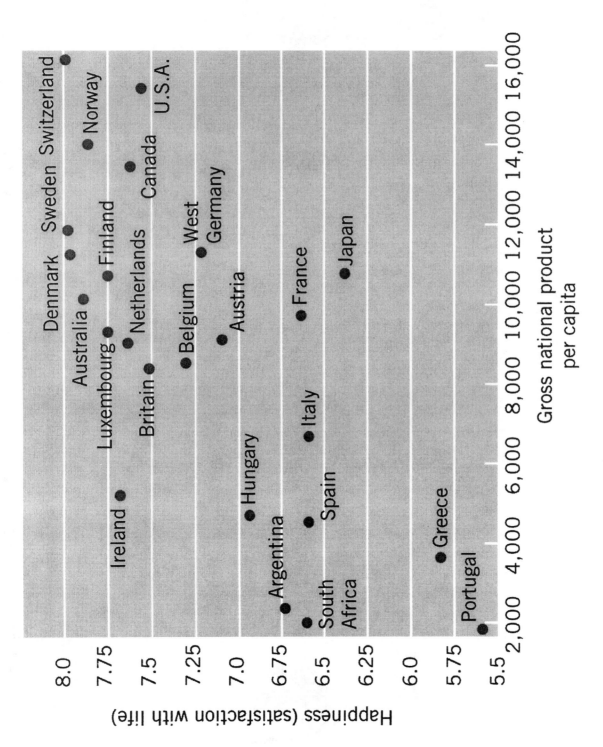

(Figure adapted from Myers & Diener, 1995, p. 13)

Westen, 2e Fig. 11.02

© 1999 John Wiley and Sons, Inc.

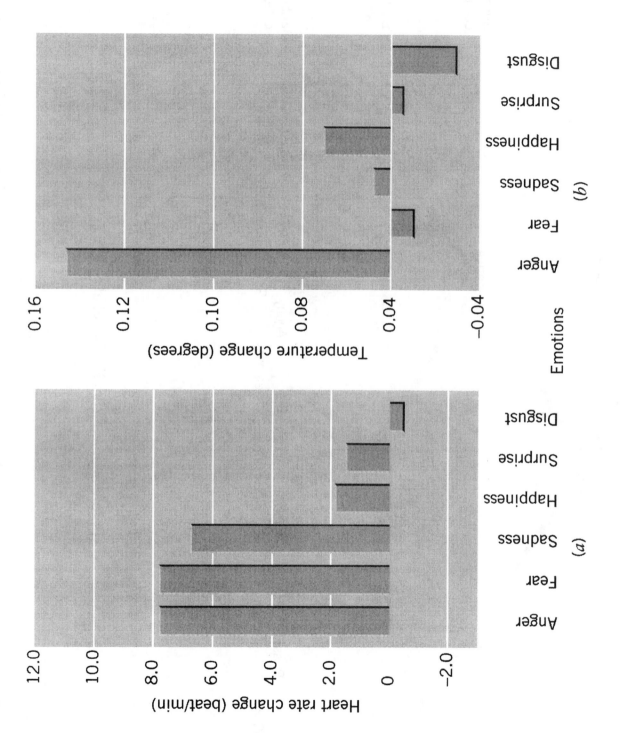

(a)

(b)

Emotions

Heart rate change (beat/min)

Temperature change (degrees)

(Figure adapted from Ekman et al., 1983, p. 1209)

Westen, 2e Fig. 11.04

© 1999 John Wiley and Sons, Inc.

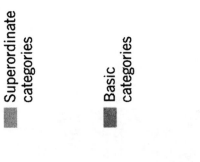

Superordinate categories

Basic categories

Subordinate categories

EMOTIONS

Positive

Negative

Love

Joy

Anger

Sadness

Fear

Fondness
Infatuation

Bliss
Contentment

Pride

Annoyance
Hostility

Contempt

Jealousy

Agony
Grief

Guilt

Loneliness

Horror

Worry

(Figure adapted from Fischer et al., 1990, p. 90)

Westen, 2e Fig. 11.06

© 1999 John Wiley and Sons, Inc.

(Figure adapted from LeDoux, 1986, p. 329)

Westen, 2e Fig. 11.07

© 1999 John Wiley and Sons, Inc.

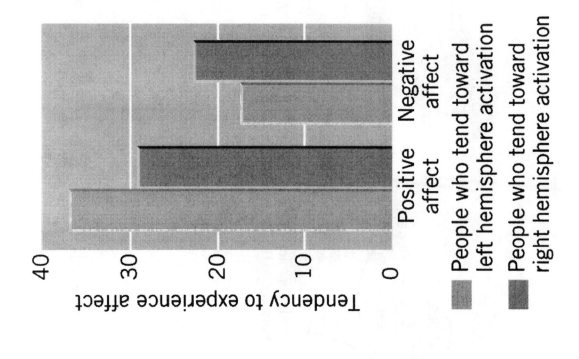

(Figure adapted from Tomarken et al., 1992, p. 681)

Westen, 2e Fig. 11.08

© 1999 John Wiley and Sons, Inc.

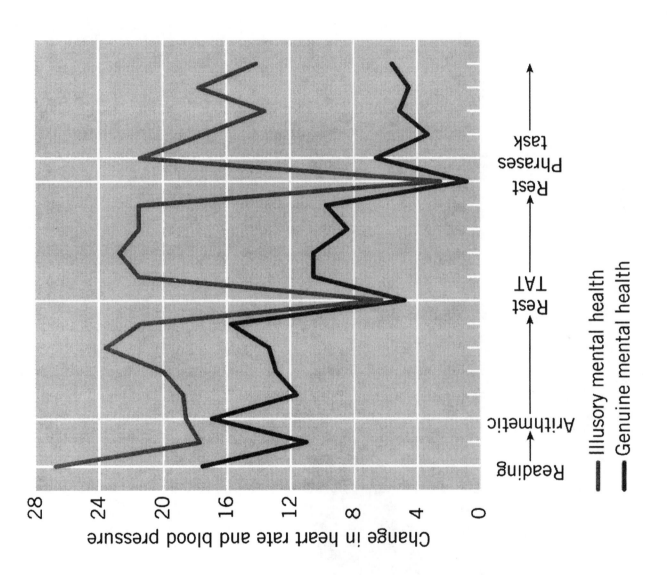

(Figure adapted from Schedler et al., 1993)

Westen, 2e Fig. 11.09

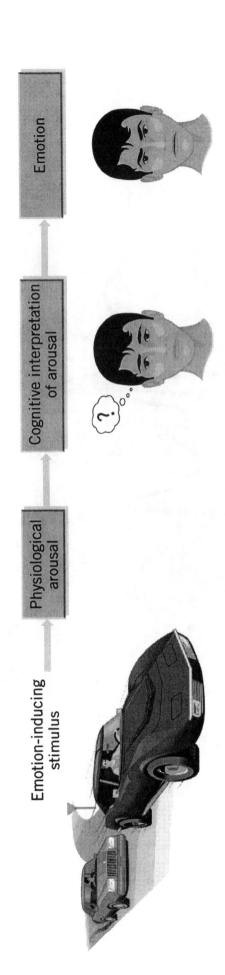

Emotion-inducing stimulus → Physiological arousal → Cognitive interpretation of arousal → Emotion

Westen, 2e Fig. 11.10

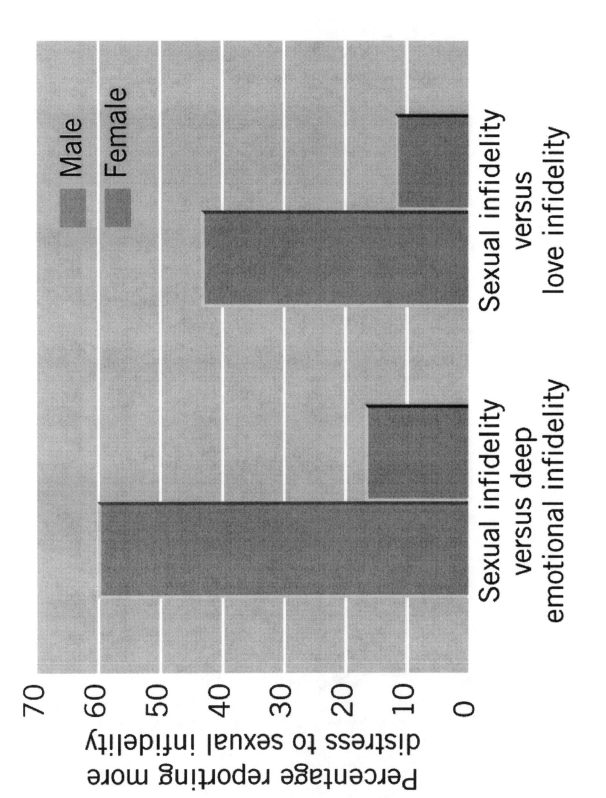

(Figure adapted from Buss et al., 1992)

Westen, 2e Fig. 11.11

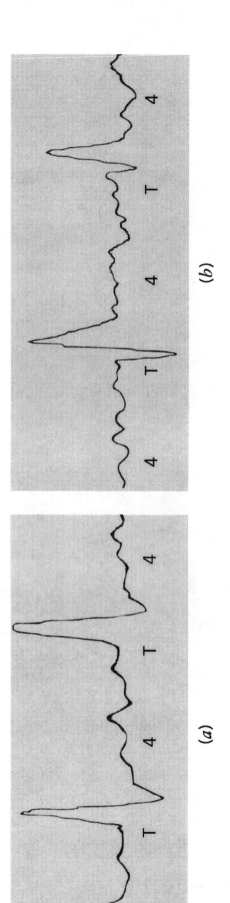

(a)

(b)

(Figure adapted from Miller, 1992)

Westen, 2e Fig. 11.12

© 1999 John Wiley and Sons, Inc.

GOAL-STATE
Representation of
ideal mother

Discrepancy

FEEDBACK
Painful emotional
state

DEFENSIVE DISTORTION
Alter conscious
view of mother

PERCEIVED REALITY
Representation of
actual mother:
often drunk

CONSCIOUS
REPRESENTATION
OF MOTHER
"Almost ideal"

Reinforcement of
defensive distortion in
similar situations

GOAL-STATE
Representation of
ideal mother

Minimized discrepancy

REDUCTION OF
AVERSIVE AFFECT

(Figure adapted from Westen, 1991)

Westen, 2e Fig. 11.13

© 1999 John Wiley and Sons, Inc.

Cause of Death	Men		Women	
	Age 35-64	Age 65-74	Age 35-64	Age 65-74
All causes	1.66	1.16	1.25	1.10
All Diseases	1.56	1.21	1.19	1.10
Cancer	1.31	1.26	1.04	1.10
Lung cancer	1.49	1.37	1.56	.98
Stomach cancer	1.49	.94	1.13	.98
Chronic heart disease	2.08	1.31	1.71	1.22
Alcohol-related illness	3.08	1.69	2.91	1.27
Motor vehicle accidents	1.52	1.05	1.52	1.22
Other accidents and violence	3.05	1.62	2.45	1.47
Suicide	3.02	2.03	2.30	.92

Source: Adapted from P. Martikainen and T. Valkenen. (1996). Mortality after the death of a spouse: Rates and causes of death in a large Finnish cohort. *American Journal of Public Health*, '86, p.1090.

Westen, 2e Fig. 11.14

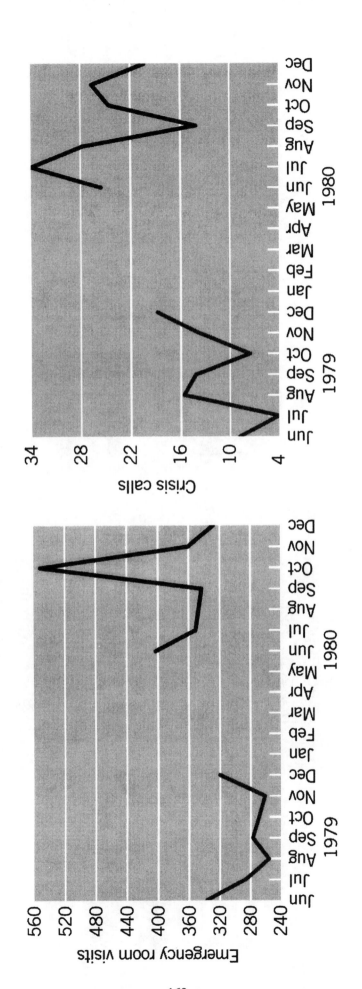

(Figure adapted from Adams & Adams, 1984, p. 257)

Westen, 2e Fig. 11.15

© 1999 John Wiley and Sons, Inc.

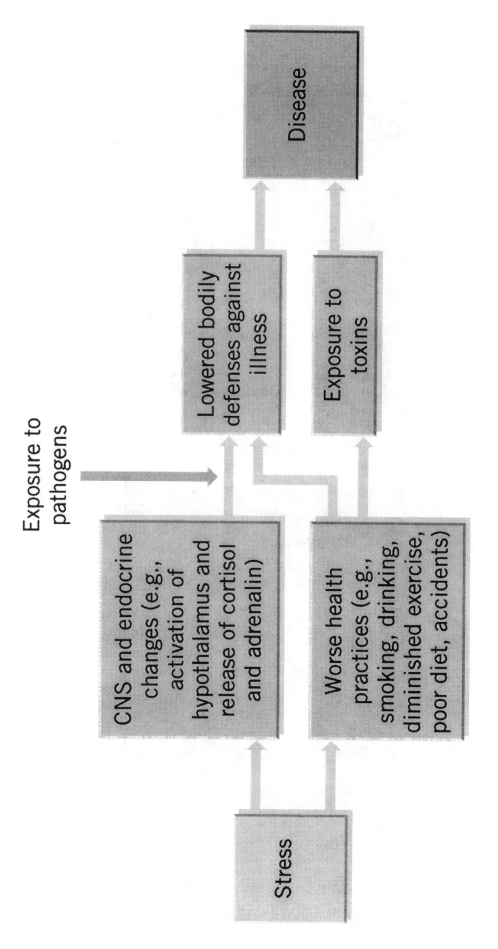

Exposure to pathogens

Stress

CNS and endocrine changes (e.g., activation of hypothalamus and release of cortisol and adrenalin)

Worse health practices (e.g., smoking, drinking, diminished exercise, poor diet, accidents)

Lowered bodily defenses against illness

Exposure to toxins

Disease

(Figure adapted from Cohen & Williamson, 1991, p.8)

Westen, 2e Fig. 11.16

© 1999 John Wiley and Sons, Inc.

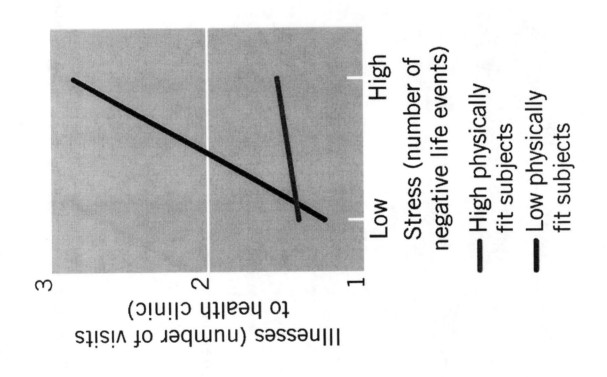

Illnesses (number of visits to health clinic)

Stress (number of negative life events)

Low   High

— High physically fit subjects

— Low physically fit subjects

(Figure adapted from Brown, 1991, p. 559)

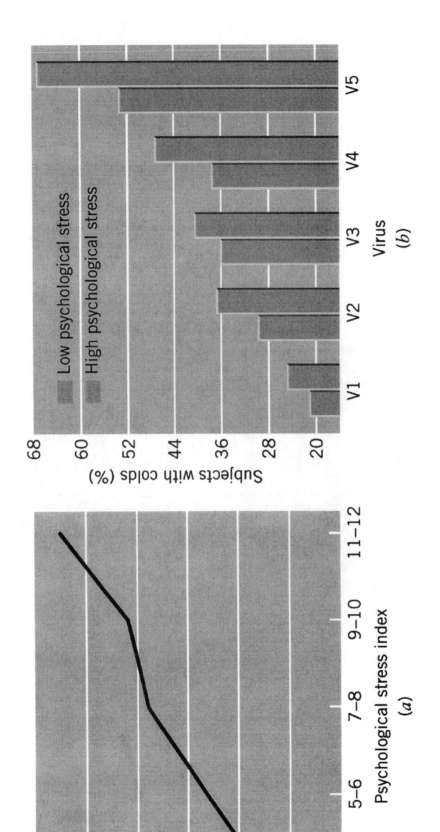

(Figure adapted from Cohen et al., 1991, pp. 609-610)

Westen, 2e Fig. 11.18

© 1999 John Wiley and Sons, Inc.

172

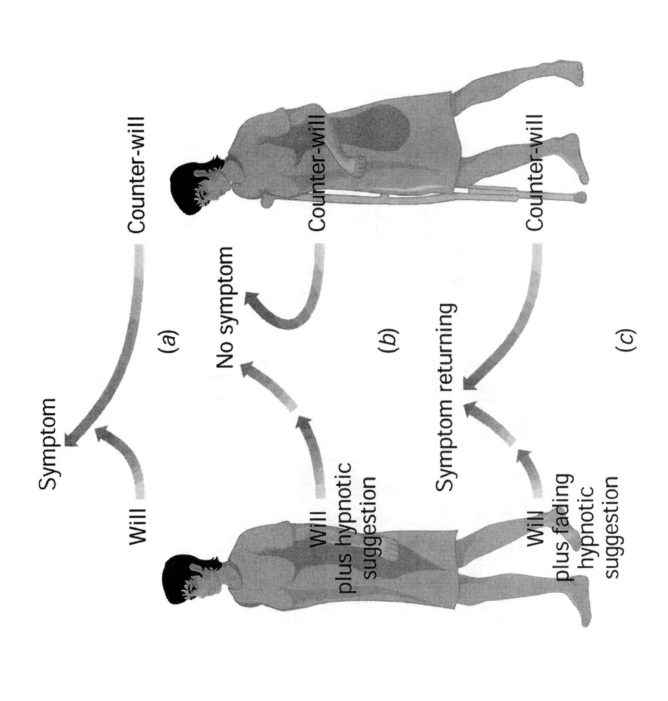

Symptom

Counter-will

Will

(a)

No symptom

Counter-will

Will
plus hypnotic
suggestion

(b)

Symptom returning

Counter-will

Will
plus fading
hypnotic
suggestion

(c)

Westen, 2e Fig. 12.01

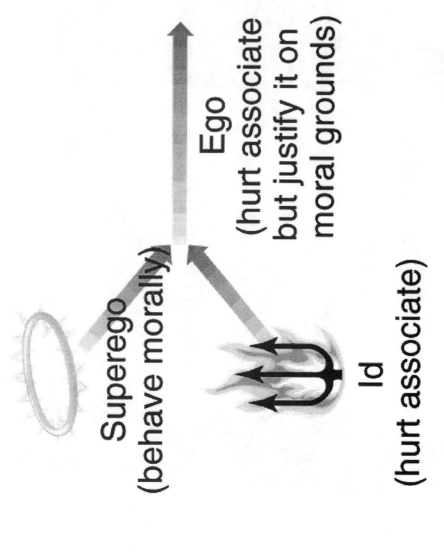

Superego
(behave morally)

Ego
(hurt associate
but justify it on
moral grounds)

Id
(hurt associate)

Encoding		Personal value		Behavior–outcome Expectancy		Competences		Self–regulation	

Stimulus

Encoding — Categorizing the event

Personal value — Relevance of the event for goals

Behavior–outcome Expectancy — Expectation that the behavior will produce the desired outcome

Behavioral plan — Formulating a plan of action

Self–efficacy expectancy — Belief in ability to execute the behavior

Competences — Skills required for executing the behavior

Behavior — Execution of plan

Self–regulation — Monitoring and adjusting behaviors and goals

Westen, 2e Fig. 12.05

© 1999 John Wiley and Sons, Inc.

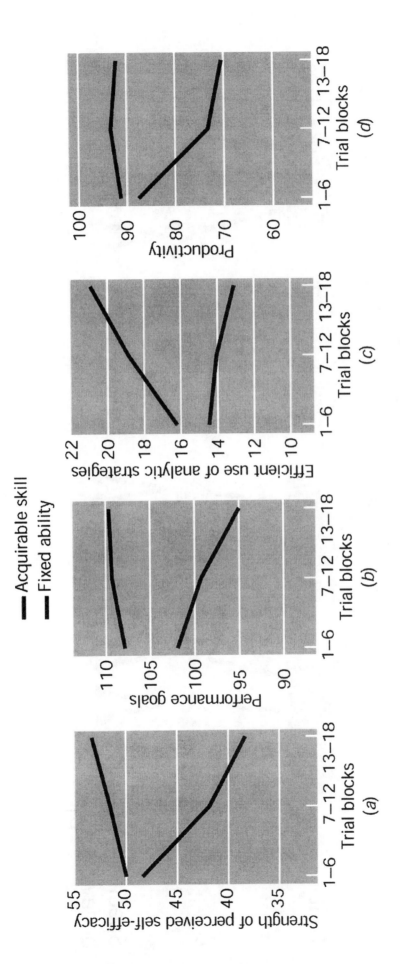

(Figure adapted from Wood & Bandura, 1989, pp. 411–413).

Westen, 2e Fig. 12.06

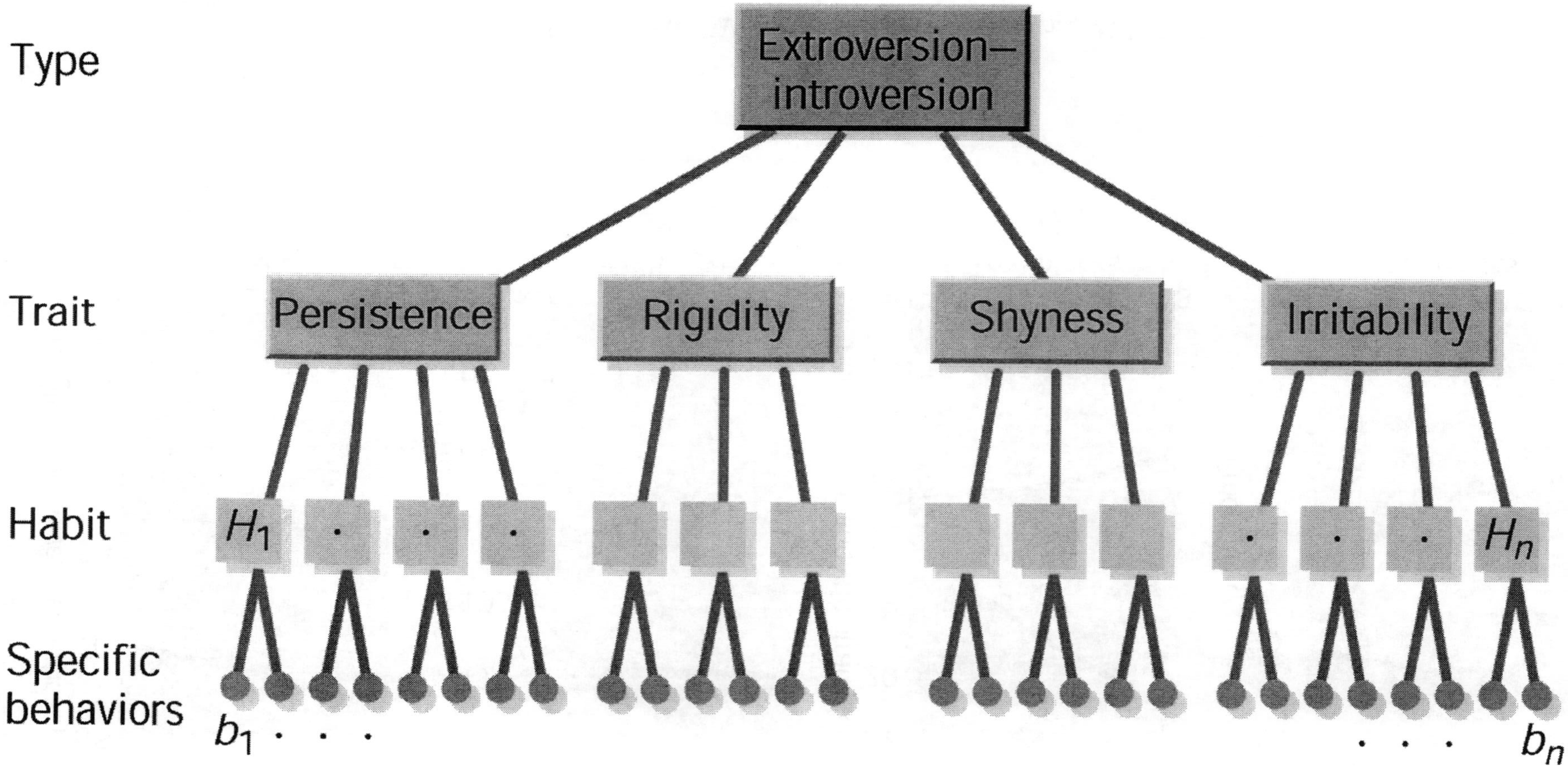

Type

Trait

Habit

Specific behaviors

(Figure adapted from Eysenck, 1953, p. 13)

Westen, 2e Fig. 12.07

© 1999 John Wiley and Sons, Inc.

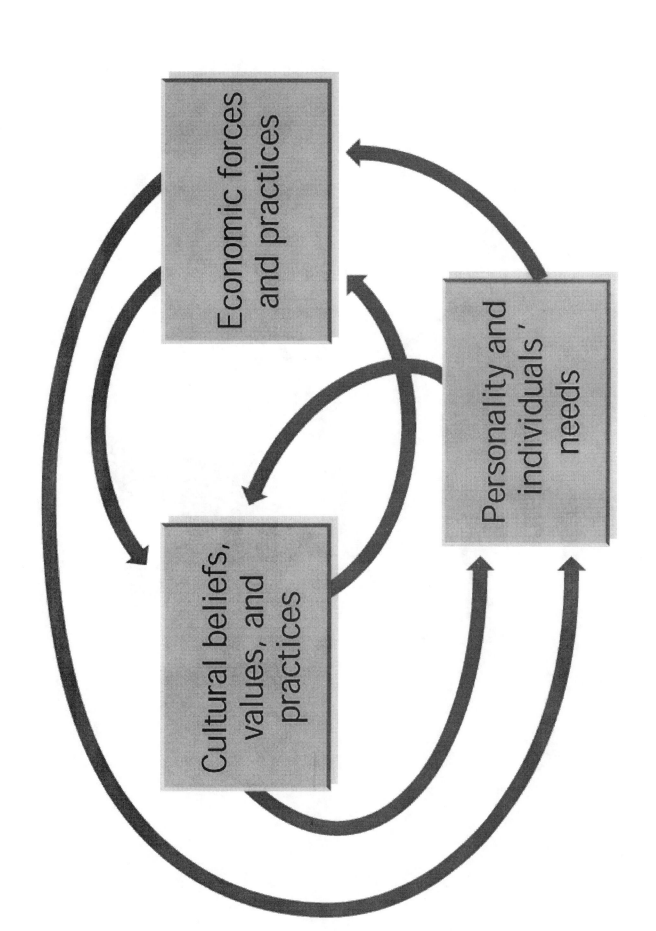

Westen, 2e Fig. 12.08

© 1999 John Wiley and Sons, Inc.

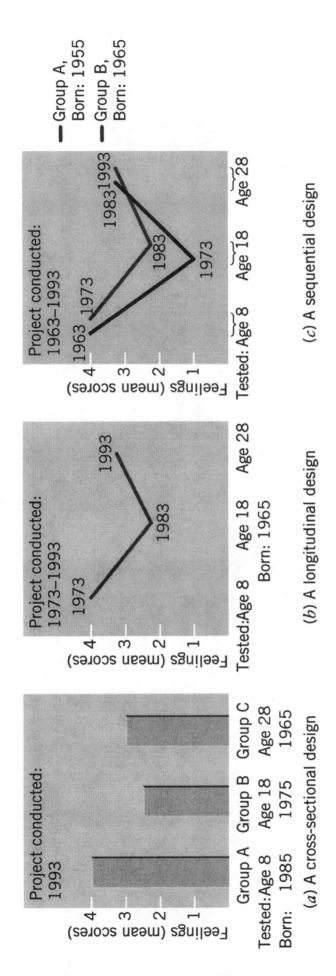

(a) A cross-sectional design

(b) A longitudinal design

(c) A sequential design

Westen, 2e Fig. 13.03

© 1999 John Wiley and Sons, Inc.

Lifts chin | Sits alone | Stands with support | Walks with support | Stands alone | Walks alone

2 months | 5 months | 6 months | 9 months | 11 months | 12 months

(Figure adapted from Frankenburg & Dodds, 1967).

Westen, 2e Fig. 13.05

© 1999 John Wiley and Sons, Inc.

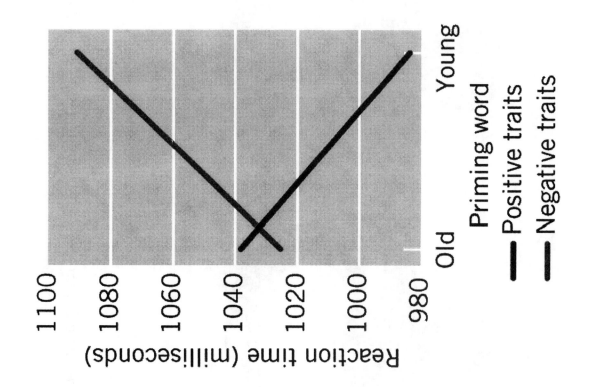

Reaction time (milliseconds)

1100 1080 1060 1040 1020 1000 980

Old   Young

Priming word

━━ Positive traits

━━ Negative traits

(Figure adapted from Perdue & Gurtman, 1990, p. 21).

Westen, 2e Fig. 13.06

(Figure adapted from Metzoff & Borton, 1979, pp. 403-404)

Westen, 2e Fig. 13.08

© 1999 John Wiley and Sons, Inc.

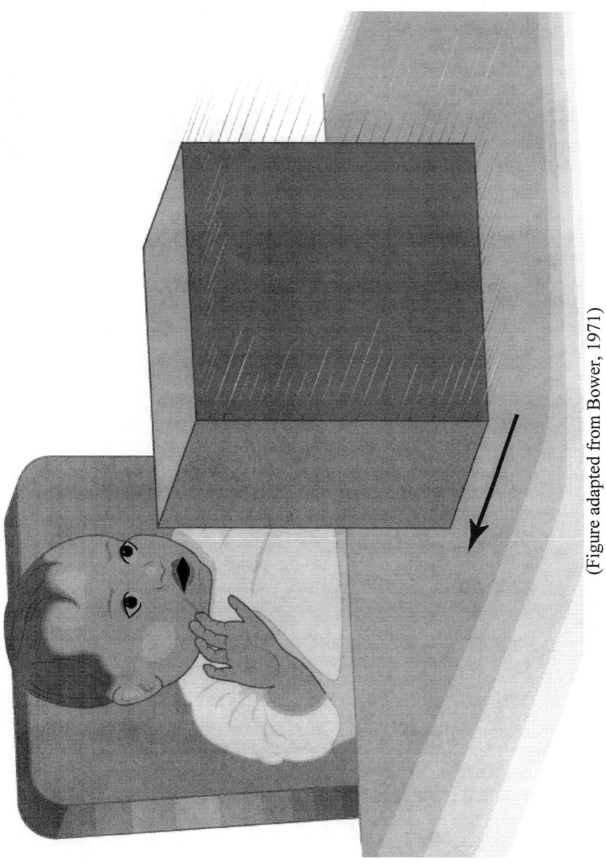

(Figure adapted from Bower, 1971)

Westen, 2e Fig. 13.09

© 1999 John Wiley and Sons, Inc.

Westen, 2e Fig. 13.10

© 1999 John Wiley and Sons, Inc.

(a) **CONSERVATION OF LIQUID QUANTITY**

Initial equality

Changed state

Conservation question:

Do the two glasses have the same amount of water, or does one glass have more than the other?

(b) **CONSERVATION OF NUMBER**

Initial equality

Changed state

Conservation question:

Do the two rows have the same number of chips, or does one row have more than the other?

(c) **CONSERVATION OF MASS**

Initial equality

Changed state

Conservation question:

Do the two pieces have the same amount of clay, or does one have more

Westen, 2e Fig. 13.11

© 1999 John Wiley and Sons, Inc.

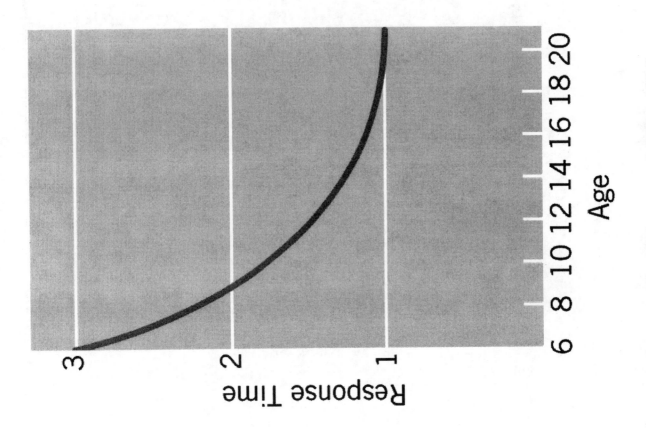

(Figure adapted from Fry & Hale, 1996)

Westen, 2e Fig. 13.12

© 1999 John Wiley and Sons, Inc.

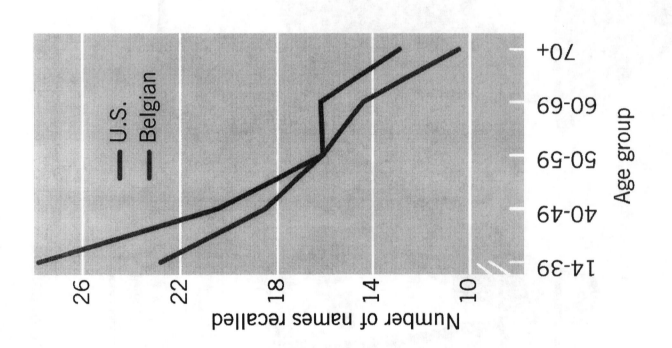

(Figure adapted from Crook et al., 1992, pp. 133)

Westen, 2e Fig. 13.14

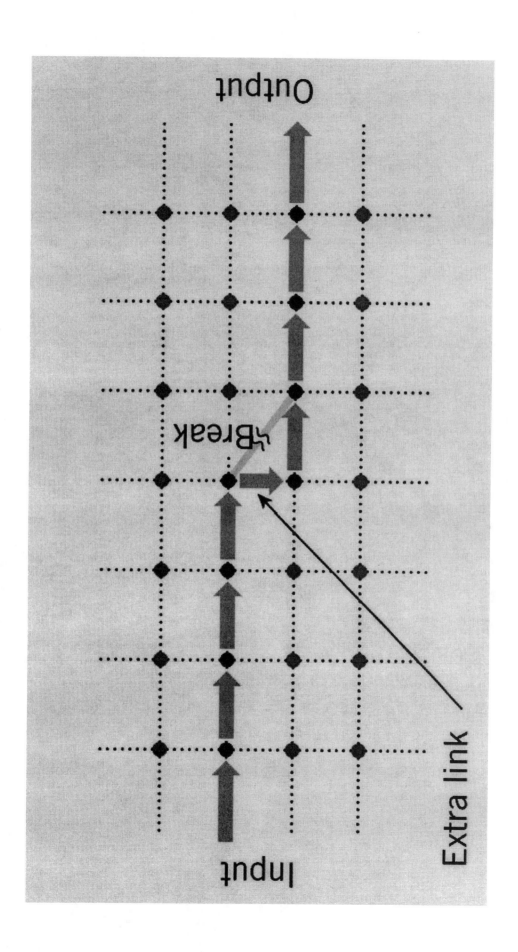

Input

Break

Extra link

(Figure adapted from Cerella, 1990, p. 203)

Westen, 2e Fig. 13.15

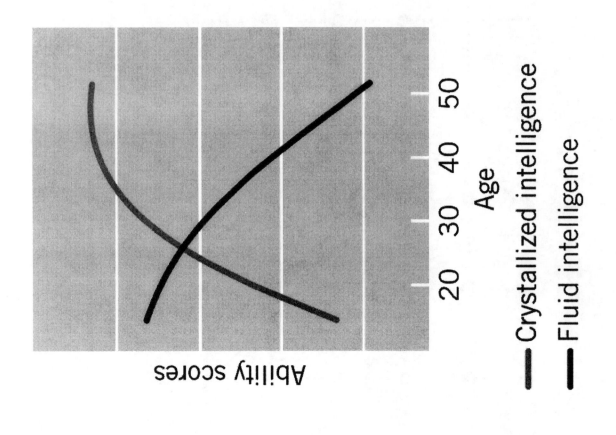

(Figure adapted from Horn & Hofer, 1992, p. 79)

Westen, 2e Fig. 13.16

© 1999 John Wiley and Sons, Inc.

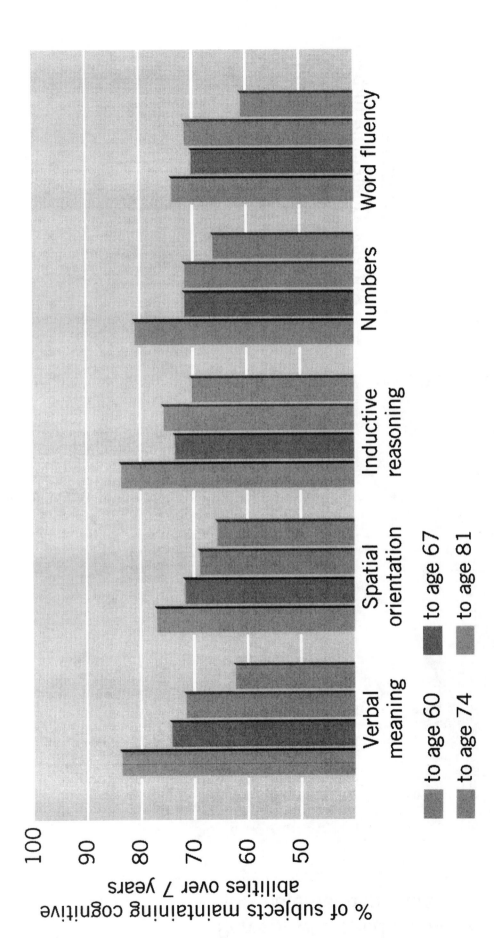

(Figure adapted from Schaie, 1990, p. 297)

Westen, 2e Fig. 13.17

© 1999 John Wiley and Sons, Inc.

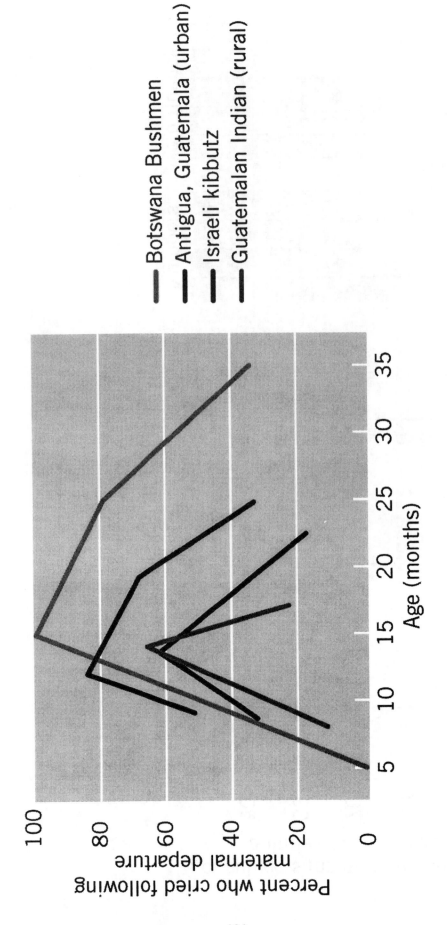

Botswana Bushmen
Antigua, Guatemala (urban)
Israeli kibbutz
Guatemalan Indian (rural)

Percent who cried following maternal departure

Age (months)

(Figure adapted from Kagan, 1983, p. 198)

© 1999 John Wiley and Sons, Inc.

Westen, 2e Fig. 14.02

My name is Bruce C. I have brown eyes. I have brown hair. I have brown eyebrows. I'm nine years old. I LOVE! sports. I have seven people in my family. I have great! eye site. I have lots of friends. I live on 1923 Pinecrest Drive. I'm going on 10 in September. I'm a boy. I have an uncle that is almost 7 feet tall. My school is Pinecrest. My teacher is Mrs. V. I play Hockey! I am almost the smartest boy in the class. I LOVE! food. I love fresh air. I LOVE school.

I am a human being. I am a girl. I am an individual. I don't know who I am. I am a Pisces. I am a moody person. I am an indecisive person. I am an ambitious person. I am a very curious person. I am not an individual. I am a loner. I am an American (God help me), I am a Democrat. I am a liberal person. I am a radical, I am a conservative. I am a pseudoliberal. I am an atheist. I am not a classifiable person (i.e., I don't want to be).

(Figure adapted from Montemayor & Eisen, 1977, pp. 317-318)

Westen, 2e Fig. 14.03

Ninth grader: In the fifth grade I was getting really bad grades and my mom yelled at me all the time and we got in big fights all the time, and before that we were real close.... The whole year and summer my mom and I were always fighting, and then in the sixth grade my mother--well, I made the honor roll and we became close again--and I was on the Student Council. And then in the eighth grade I got Ds and Cs and we were fighting a lot but after graduation from middle school we were close again, and this year I was on the honor roll first quarter, and then last quarter I got 3 Cs and 3 Bs and she's yelling at me again, and we're not as close as before.

Twelfth grader: As I'm getting older we argue more, disagree on more--disagree on a lot more things. But I think we're getting closer now, more on the same level than when I was a little girl. Like, one time I was getting ready for a competition--we had a lot of misunderstanding, beforehand--I didn't feel she understood. She'd been in so many of these competitions and won, and I didn't feel she really cared about this one I was in. She hadn't felt I was serious about it. I didn't think she cared, and she didn't think I was serious. So finally we talked about it--realized it was a misunder-standing. I think we're closer now--I realized we do have to talk about things when we have misunderstandings.

(Figure adapted from Westen et al., 1991)

Westen, 2e Fig. 14.04

© 1999 John Wiley and Sons, Inc.

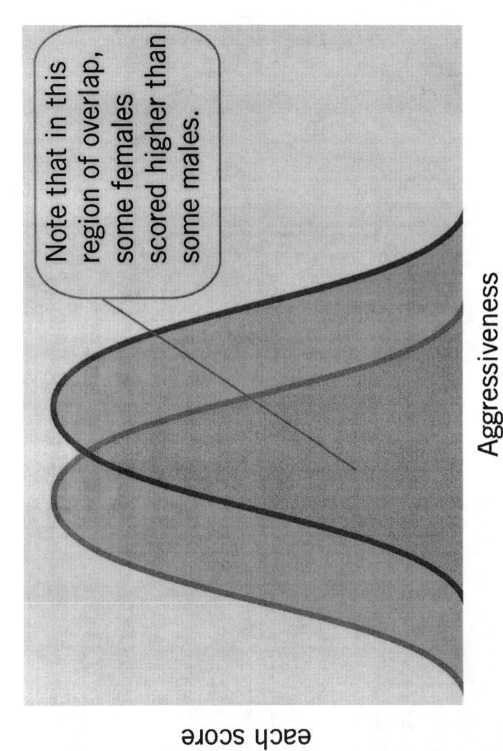

Aggressiveness

—— Average score for females
—— Average score for males

Note that in this region of overlap, some females scored higher than some males.

Number of participants receiving each score

© 1999 John Wiley and Sons, Inc.

Westen, 2e Fig. 14.05

CAUSE

Did the person cause the damage? Did his actions contribute to it in some way?

MORAL RESPONSIBILITY

Did he intend to do harm? Was he reckless or negligent? Should he have foreseen it?

BLAME

Was the harm substantial? Was it justified for any reason?

NO PUNISHMENT

PUNISHMENT

How much damage was done? Has the perpetrator made restitution or suffered from his action?

(Figure adapted from Darley & Schultz, 1990, p. 532).

Westen, 2e Fig. 14.06

© 1999 John Wiley and Sons, Inc.

TABLE 14.5 Erikson's Psychological Stages in Relation to Other Models of Development

Life Period	Erikson's Psychosocial Stage	Freud's Psychosexual Stage	Piaget's Cognitive Stage
Infancy	*Basic trust versus mistrust:* Development of interpersonal expectations and hope	Oral	Sensorimotor
Toddlerhood	*Autonomy versus shame and doubt:* Development of will and self-control	Anal	Preoperational
Preschool and early school years	*Initiative versus guilt:* Development of conscience and purpose	Phallic	
Late childhood	*Industry versus inferiority:* Development of competence	Latency	Concrete operational
Adolescence	*Identity versus identity confusion:* Development of commitment and sense of integration	Genital	Formal operational
Young adulthood	*Intimacy versus isolation:* Development of adult love		
Midlife	*Generativity versus stagnation:* Development of care for the next generation and for one's legacy		
Old age	*Integrity versus despair:* Development of wisdom		

Note: Erikson's model describes psychosocial development, which is not independent of either the development of pleasure-seeking motives, as described by Freud, or cognition, as described by Piaget. Among the major theories we have discussed, however, Erikson's is the only one that posits development through adulthood.

Westen, 2e Table. 14.05

LEVEL OF DISTURBANCE	CAPACITIES		
	Love	Work	Relation to Reality
Normal to neurotic	Able to maintain relationships.	Able to maintain employment.	Able to see reality clearly.
	May have minor difficulties such as conflicts with significant others or a tendency to be competitive.	May have difficulties such as rigidity, defensiveness, underconfidence, workaholism, overambition, or underachievement.	May have minor defensive distortions, such as seeing the self and significant others as better than they really are.
Personality disordered	Unable to maintain relationships consistently.	Difficulty maintaining employment.	Generally able to see reality with clarity (i.e., with no hallucinations or delusions).
	May avoid relationships, jump into them too quickly, or end them abruptly.	May be grossly underemployed, extremely unable to get along with bosses, or likely to terminate employment abruptly.	Prone to gross misinterpretations in interpersonal affairs. (A subset suffers from chronically idiosyncratic thinking.)
Psychotic	Tremendous difficulty maintaining relationships. Isolated.	Unable to maintain employment anywhere near intellectual level.	Unable to distinguish clearly between what is real and what is not.
	May be socially peculiar.	Large percentage are chronically unemployed.	Has delusions, hallucinations, or other psychotic thought processes.

Westen, 2e Fig. 15.01

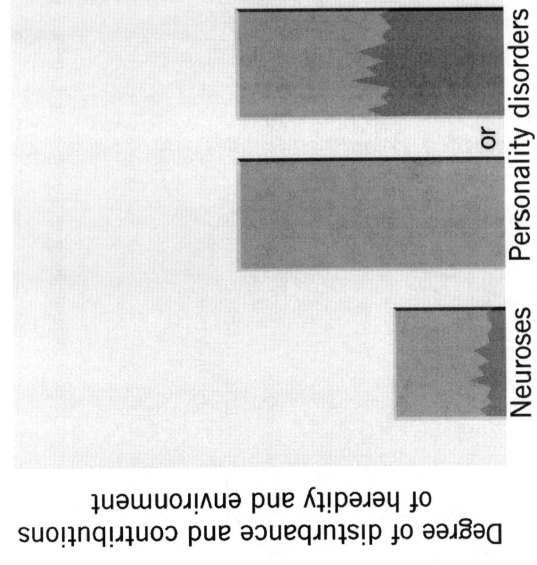

Neuroses   Personality disorders   Psychoses

or

Experiences, particularly in childhood

Heredity

Degree of disturbance and contributions of heredity and environment

Westen, 2e Fig. 15.02

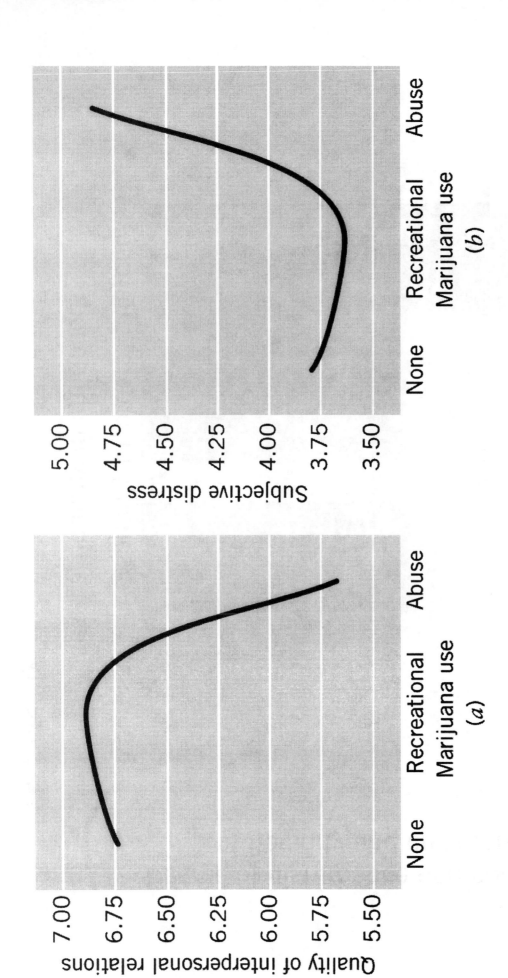

(Figure adapted from Shedler & Block, 1990, p. 624)

Westen, 2e Fig. 15.03

© 1999 John Wiley and Sons, Inc.

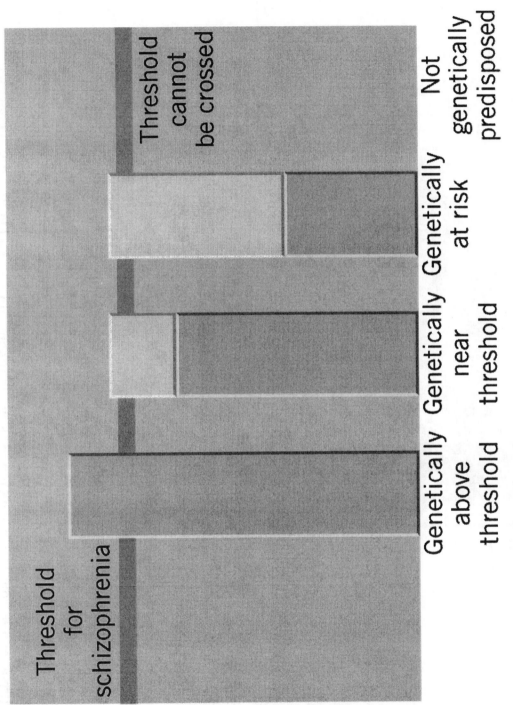

Genetic and environmental contributions needed to cross threshold

Threshold for schizophrenia

Threshold cannot be crossed

Genetically above threshold

Genetically near threshold

Genetically at risk

Not genetically predisposed

■ Genetic vulnerability

□ Environmental component necessary to cross threshold

Westen, 2e Fig. 15.05

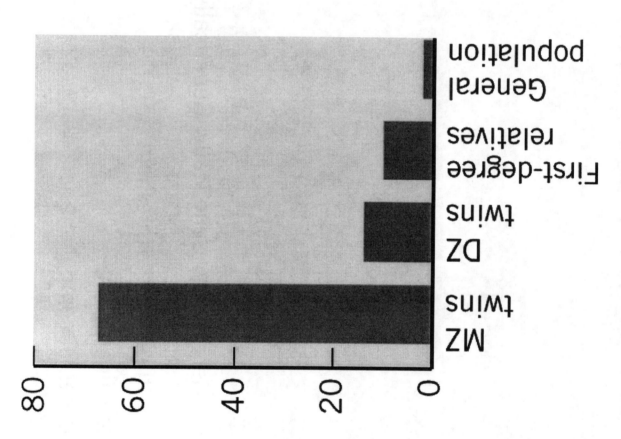

(Figure adapted from D.F. MacKinnon, K.R. Jamison, and J.R. DeDavlo (1997) Genetics of manic-depressive illness. Annual Review of Neuroscience, 20, 355-373.)

Westen, 2e Fig. 15.07

© 1999 John Wiley and Sons, Inc.

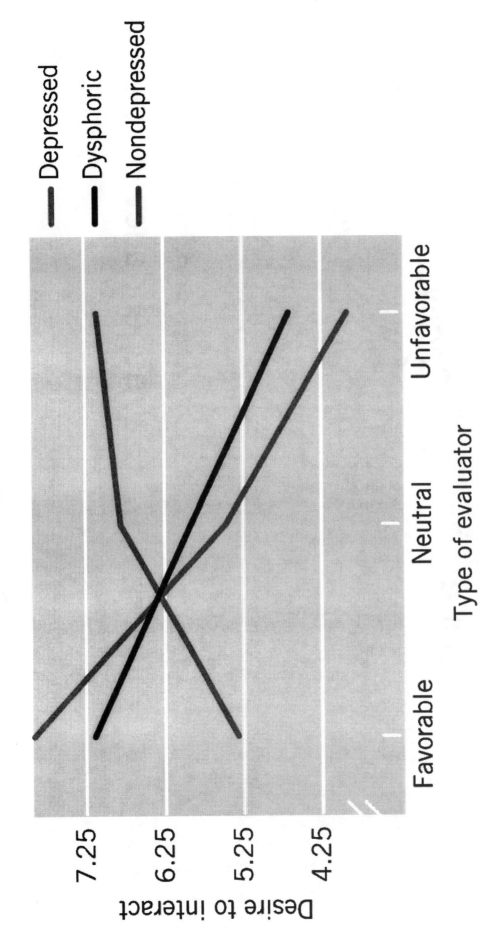

(Figure adapted from Swann et al., 1992, p. 296)

Westen, 2e Fig. 15.08

© 1999 John Wiley and Sons, Inc.

(Figure adapted from Beck, 1976, p 256)

Westen, 2e Fig. 15.09

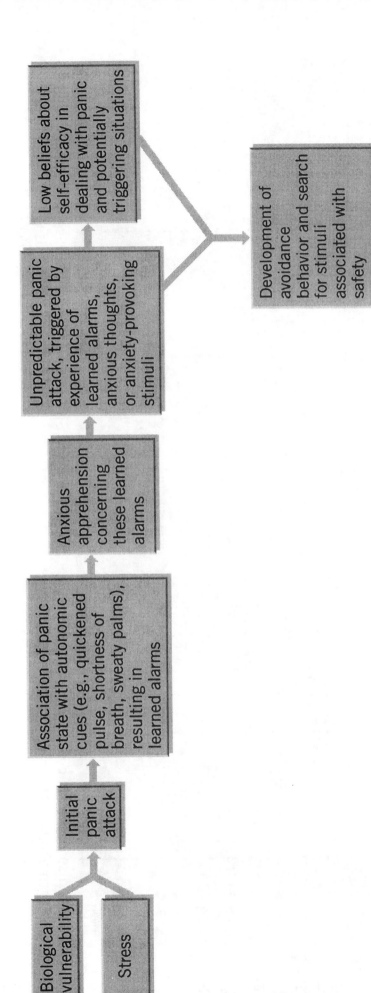

Westen, 2e Fig. 15.10

© 1999 John Wiley and Sons, Inc.

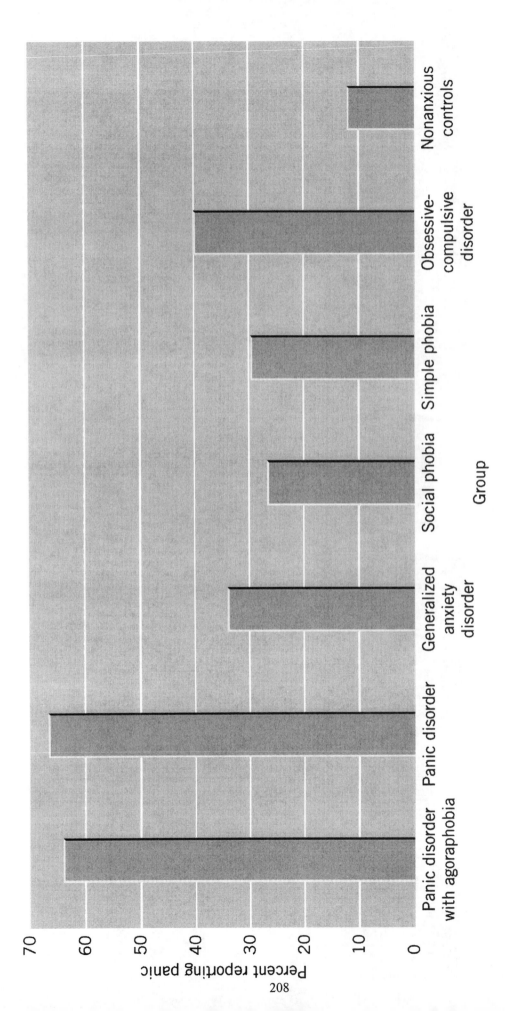

(Figure adapted from Rapee et al., 1992, p. 545)

Westen, 2e Fig. 15.11

© 1999 John Wiley and Sons, Inc.

| | Aggressivity in adoptee (% of participants) | |
	No	Yes
Antisocial personality disorder in biological parent No	84	16
Yes	52	48

(Figure adapted from Cadoret, et al., (1995). Adoption study demonstrating two genetic pathways to drug abuse. Archives of General Psychiatry, 52, p.48)

Westen, 2e Fig. 15.12

© 1999 John Wiley and Sons, Inc.

Loretta was a woman in her late 30s who sought treatment for long-standing anxiety and depression and an unsatisfying sexual relationship with her husband. Loretta came from a very conservative religious family and described her father as aloof and her mother as extremely critical. In the excerpt below, she describes feeling more relaxed with men, an exciting but still unsettling feeling:

Therapist: How would you experience men before you started feeling this way?

Patient: Sort of avoidance. I didn't—difficulty relating to them. . . .

Therapist: Is that different now?

Patient: It's a little different now. In fact, I've noticed it. I can even encounter somebody, a man. . . and I can joke and cut up, and sort of banter back and forth, which has always been a real problem for me. . . .

Therapist: It sounds like you have started to feel more comfortable with men. What's bothersome then?

Patient: Well, I guess it's the whole thing of sexual interest, I guess. . . [T]hat part of me that was always taught that sex and intimacy and physicalness was reserved for someone you were very bound to, and were going to spend the rest of your life with. That sort of thing.

Therapist: That sounds like you still believe that. We are talking about your curiosity.

Patient: Well, when I'm in a situation where I'm with a man, with the person I'm supposed to spend my life with, and I should not be having all these sexual feelings about other men. . . .

Therapist: Well, do you think that is pretty common?

Patient: Well, this friend I have, she feels the same way and she and I have had a lot of discussions about that.

Therapist: Then, there are two of you walking around.

Patient: There are two of us. (Laughs)

(Figure adapted from Strupp & Binder, 1984)

Westen, 2e Fig. 16.01

Sitting behind the wheel of a nonmoving car in the driveway.

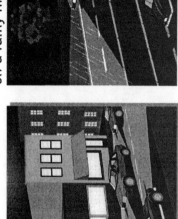

Driving along a busy street on a sunny day.

Driving on the same street at night.

Driving on a busy expressway on a rainy night.

Driving on a busy expressway in the daytime.

Driving on the same street in the rain.

Driving along an empty, quiet street on a sunny day.

Least   1   2   3   4   5   6   7   Most

Amount of anxiety

Westen, 2e Fig. 16.02

© 1999 John Wiley and Sons, Inc.

211

1 What is my problem?

2 How can I do it?

3 Am I using my plan?

4 How did I do?

(Figure adapted from Camp & Bash, 1981)

Westen, 2e Fig. 16.03

© 1999 John Wiley and Sons, Inc.

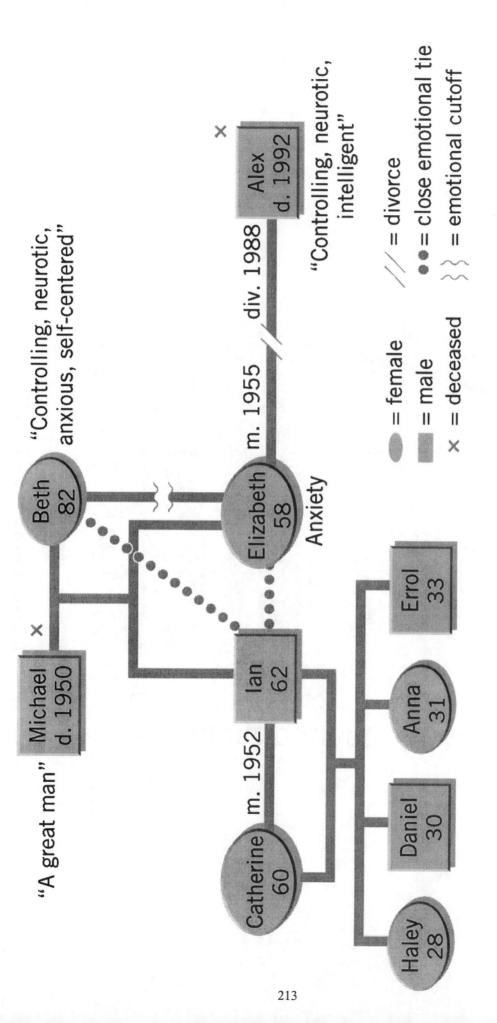

"A great man"

"Controlling, neurotic, anxious, self-centered"

"Controlling, neurotic, intelligent"

Beth
82

Michael
d. 1950

Elizabeth
58

Anxiety

Alex
d. 1992

m. 1955   div. 1988

Ian
62

Catherine   m. 1952
60

Errol
33

Anna
31

Daniel
30

Haley
28

= female

= male

= deceased

// = divorce

= close emotional tie

= emotional cutoff

Westen, 2e Fig. 16.04

© 1999 John Wiley and Sons, Inc.

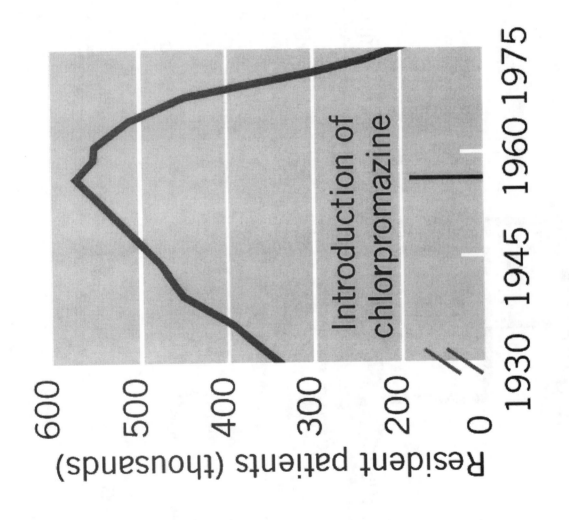

(Figure adapted from Davis, 1985)

Westen, 2e Fig. 16.05

(a) Decreases neural transmission by "locking up" receptor sites

Neurotransmitters released

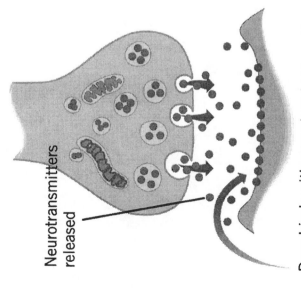

Drug binds with receptors to prevent them from being activated by the neurotransmitters in the synapse.

(b) Increases neural transmission by blocking reuptake

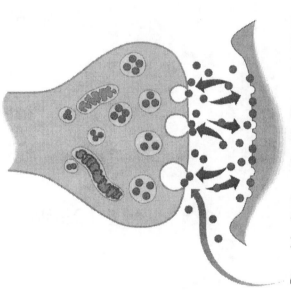

Drug blocks neurotransmitters from being taken back into the presynaptic membrane, leaving the neurotransmitters in the synapse longer.

(c) Increases neural transmission by blocking breakdown of neurotransmitters in synaptic vesicles

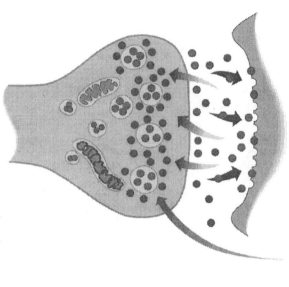

Drug prevents the neurotransmitter returning from the synapse from being broken down for storage, which keeps it available at the synapse.

Westen, 2e Fig. 16.06

© 1999 John Wiley and Sons, Inc.

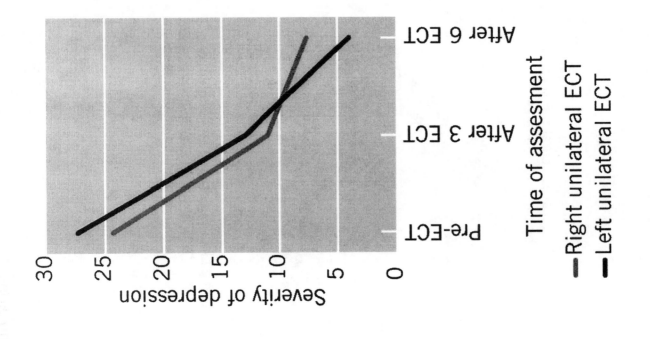

(Figure adapted from Abrams et al., 1989)

Westen, 2e Fig. 16.07

© 1999 John Wiley and Sons, Inc.

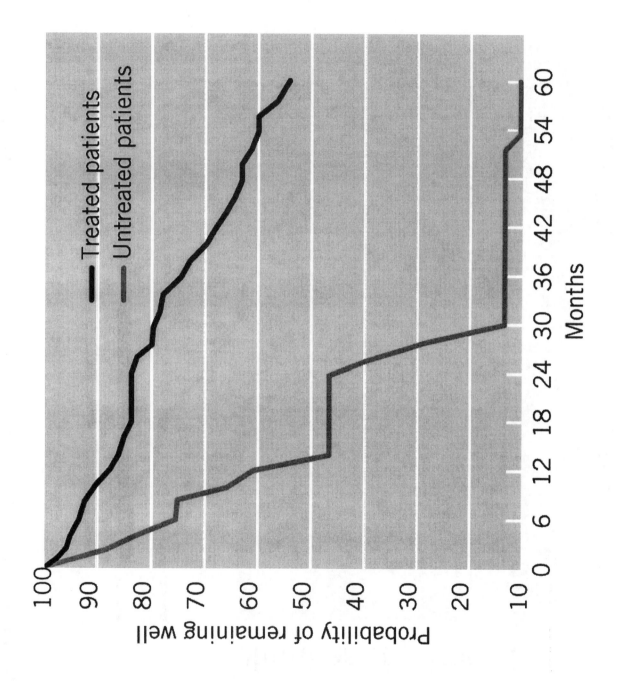

(Figure adapted from Maj et al., 1992)

Westen, 2e Fig. 16.08

© 1999 John Wiley and Sons, Inc.

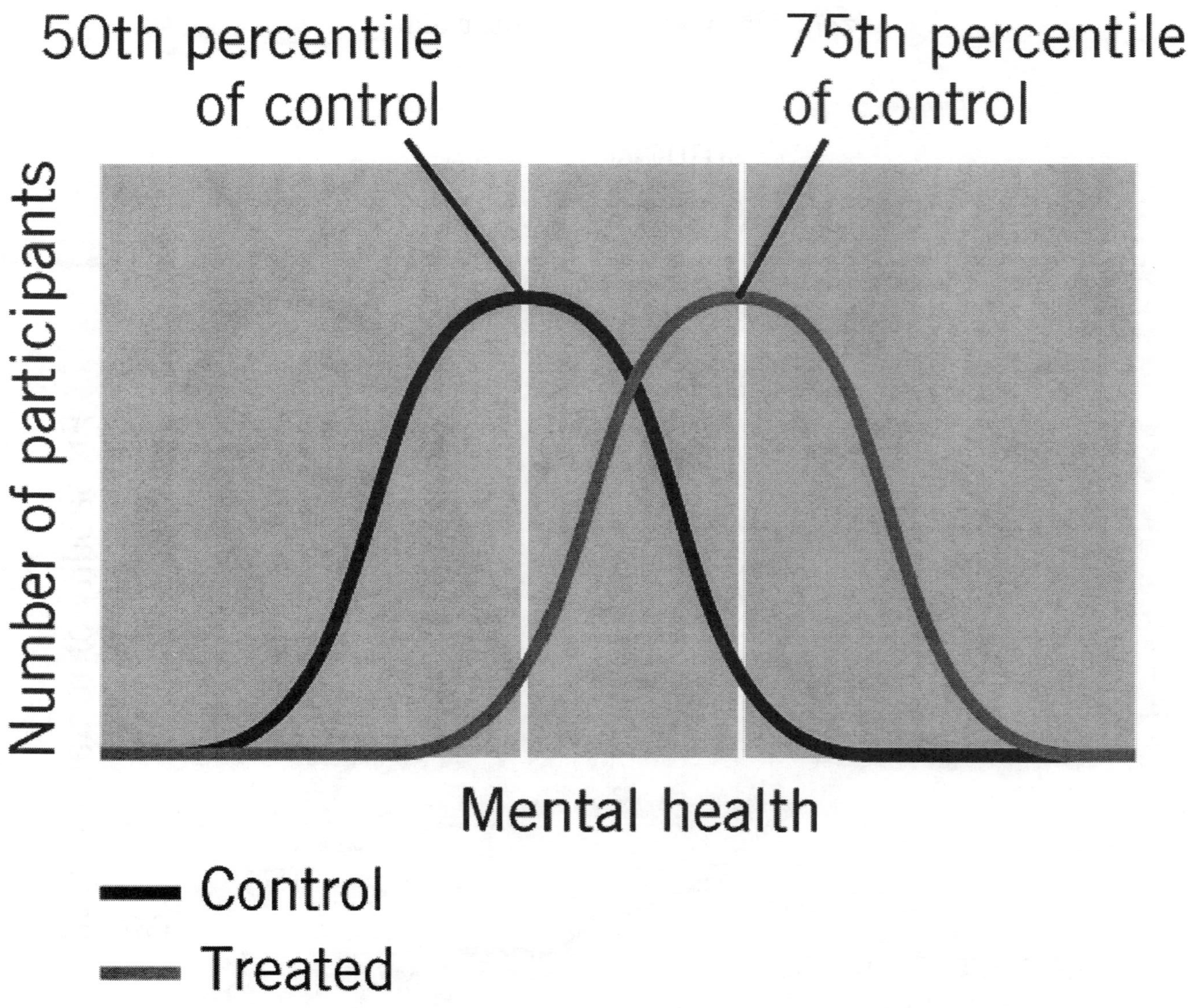

75th percentile of control

50th percentile of control

Mental health

Number of participants

— Control
— Treated

(Figure adapted from Smith & Glass, 1977)

Westen, 2e Fig. 16.09

© 1999 John Wiley and Sons, Inc.

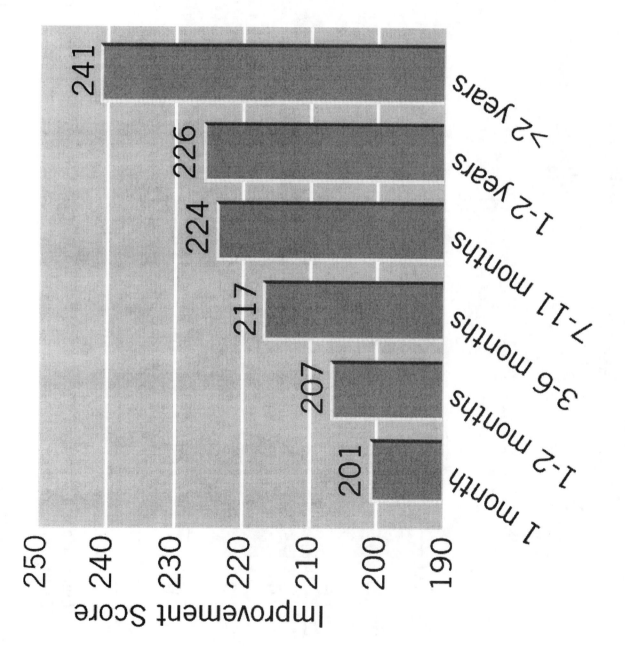

(Figure adapted from Seligman, 1995, p. 968)

Westen, 2e Fig. 16.10

© 1999 John Wiley and Sons, Inc.

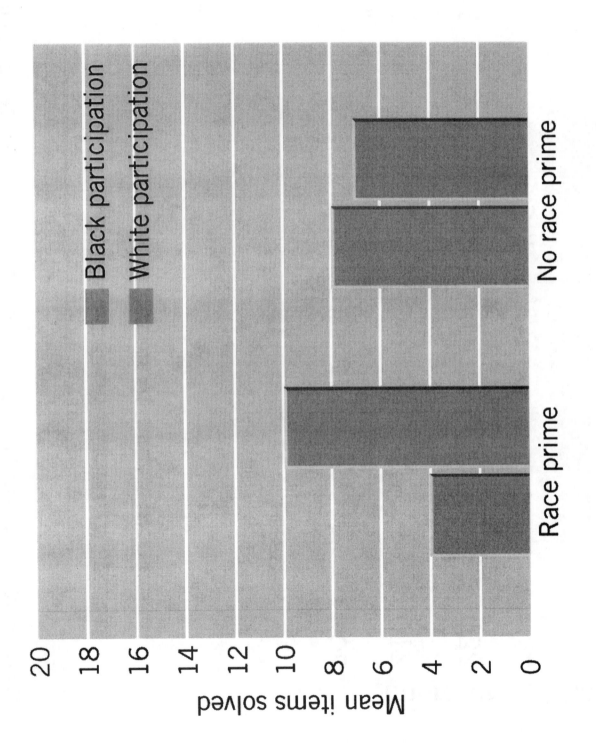

(Figure adapted from C.M. Steele (1997) A threat in the air: How stereotypes shape intellectual identity and performance. American Psychologist. 52, p. 621)

Westen, 2e Fig. 17.01

© 1999 John Wiley and Sons, Inc.

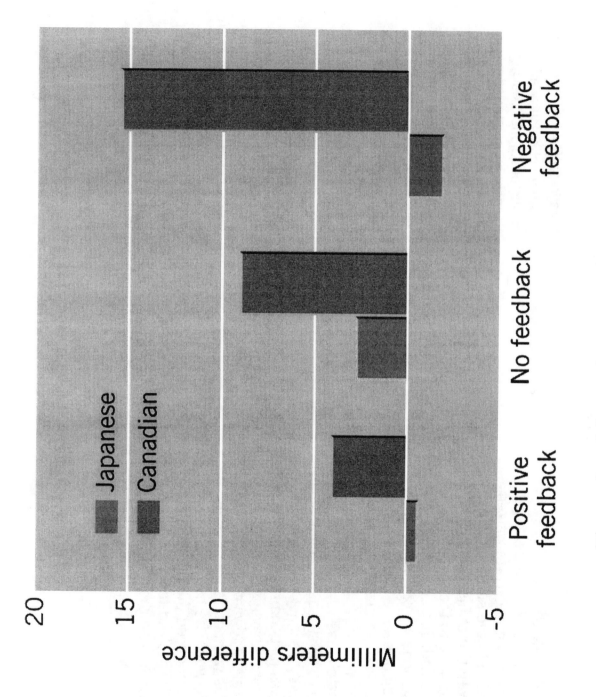

(Figure adapted from Heine &
Lehman, 1997, p 396)

Westen, 2e Fig. 17.02

© 1999 John Wiley and Sons, Inc.

Paragraph A

Jim left the house to get some stationery. He walked out into the sun-filled street with two of his friends, basking in the sun as he walked. Jim entered the stationery store, which was full of people. Jim talked with an acquaintance while he waited for the clerk to catch his eye. On his way out, he stopped to chat with a school friend who was just coming into the store. Leaving the store, he walked toward school. On his way out he met the girl to whom he had been introduced the night before. They talked for a short while, and then Jim left for school.

Paragraph B

After school Jim left the classroom alone. Leaving the school, he started on his long walk home. The street was brilliantly filled with sunshine. Jim walked down the street on the shady side. Coming down the street toward him, he saw the pretty girl whom he had met on the previous evening. Jim crossed the street and entered a candy store. The store was crowded with students, and he noticed a few familiar faces. Jim waited quietly until the counterman caught his eye and then gave his order. Taking his drink, he sat down at a side table. When he had finished his drink he went home.

(Figure adapted from Luchins, 1957, pp. 34-35)

Westen, 2e Fig. 17.03

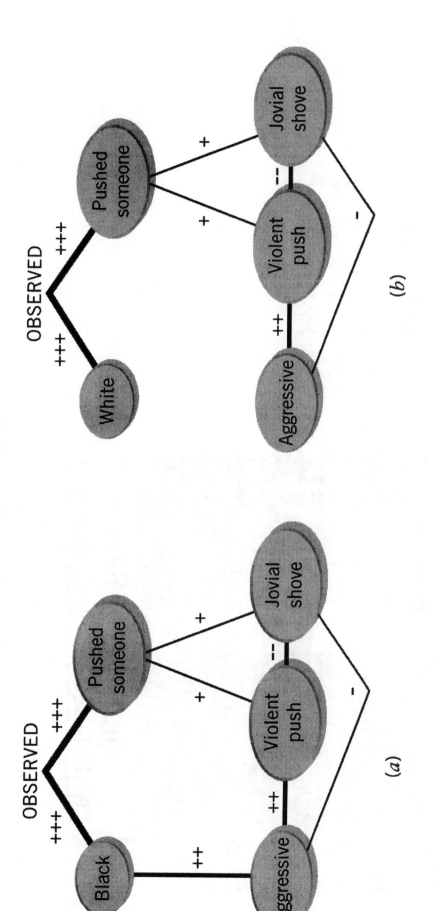

(a)

(b)

(Figure adapted from Z. Kunda & P. Thagard (1996) Forming impressions from stereotypes, traits, and behaviors: A parallel-constraint-satisfaction theory. Psych. Review, 103, p 286)

Westen, 2e Fig. 17.04

© 1999 John Wiley and Sons, Inc.

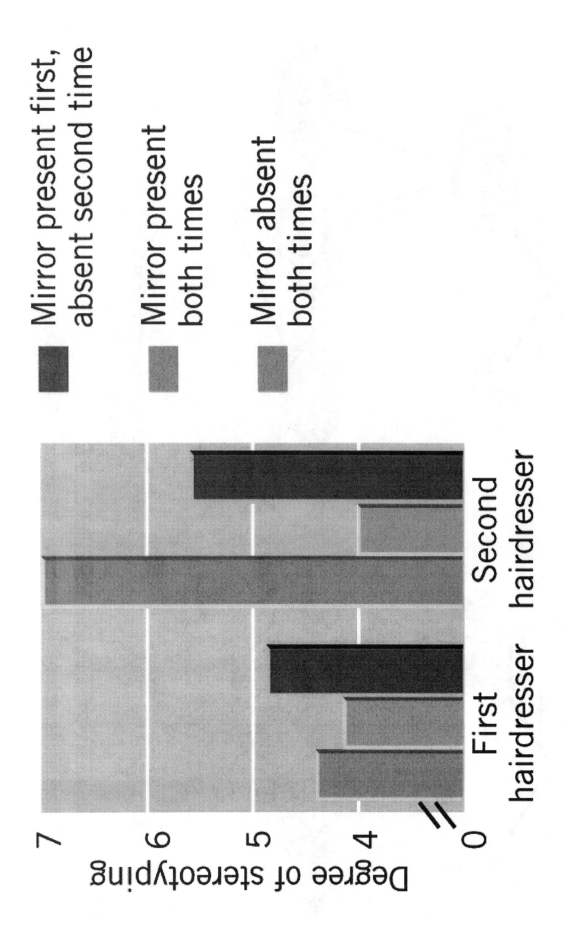

(Figure adapted from Macrae et al., 1998)

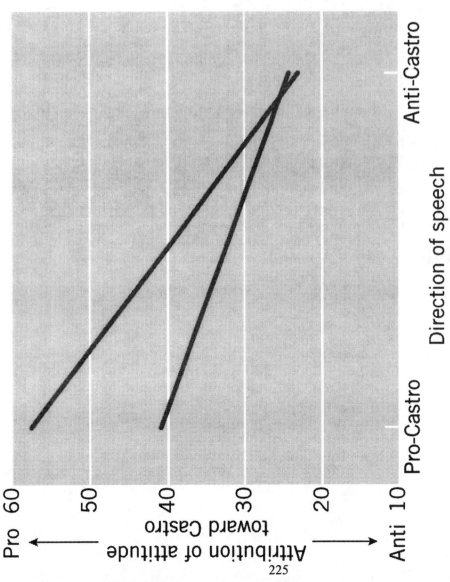

— Participants who were told the speaker was expressing his own opinion

— Participants who were told the speaker was instructed which position to take

Anti-Castro

Direction of speech

Pro-Castro

Pro 60

50

40

30

20

Anti 10

Attribution of attitude toward Castro

(Figure adapted from Jones, 1976, p. 301)

Westen, 2e Fig. 17.06

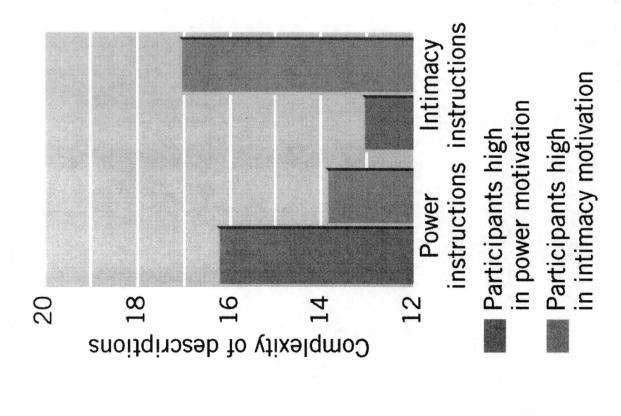

Complexity of descriptions

20

18

16

14

12

Power
instructions

Intimacy
instructions

■ Participants high
in power motivation

■ Participants high
in intimacy motivation

(Figure adapted from Woike & Aronoff, 1992, p. 102)

Westen, 2e Fig. 17.07

© 1999 John Wiley and Sons, Inc.

226

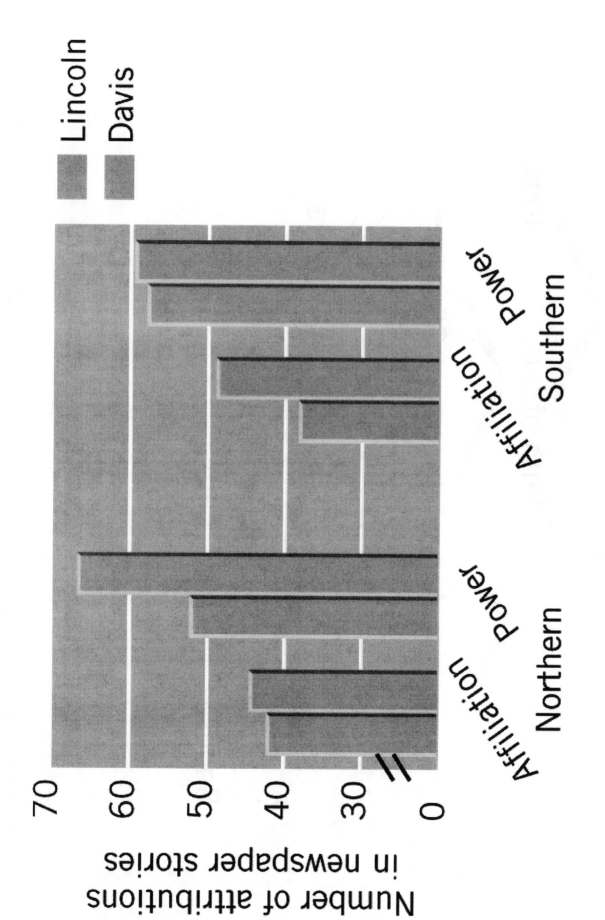

(Figure adapted from Winter, 1987, p. 44)

Westen, 2e Fig. 17.08

© 1999 John Wiley and Sons, Inc.

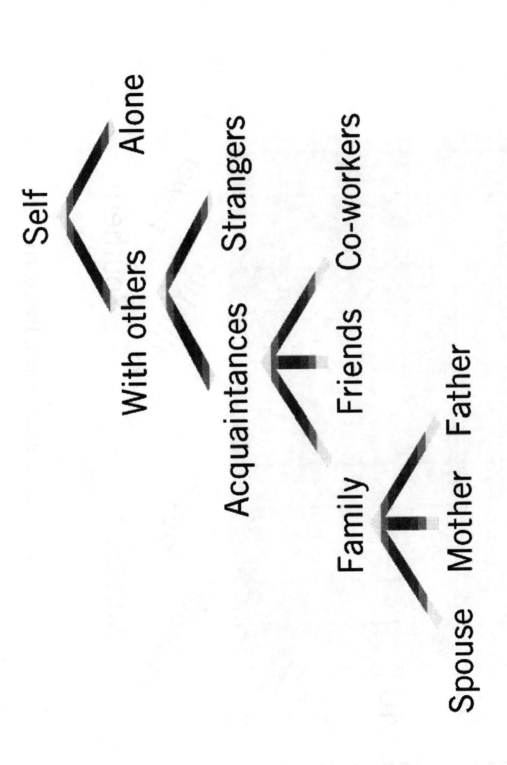

(Figure adapted from Kihlstrom & Cantor, 1983)

Westen, 2e Fig. 17.09

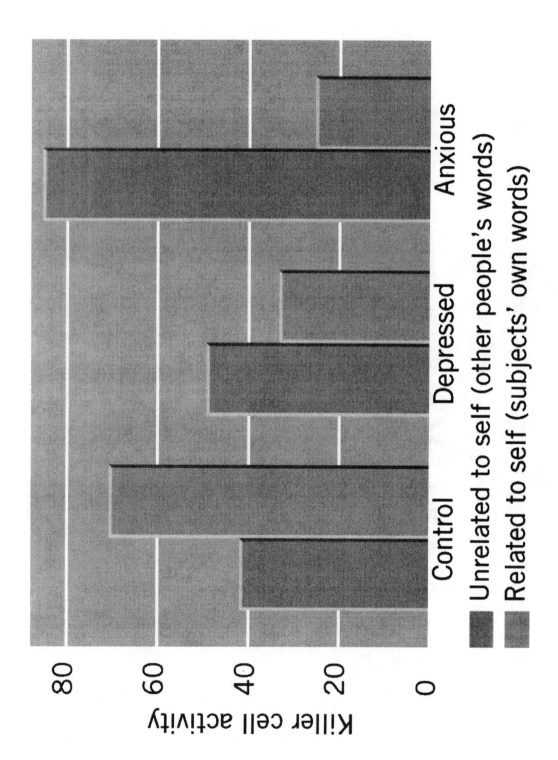

Killer cell activity

Control   Depressed   Anxious

- ■ Unrelated to self (other people's words)
- ▨ Related to self (subjects' own words)

(Figure adapted from Strauman et al., 1993, p. 1049)

Westen, 2e Fig. 17.10

© 1999 John Wiley and Sons, Inc.

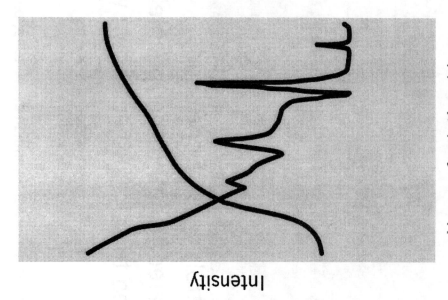

Intensity

Years of relationship
— Passionate love
— Companionate love

Westen, 2e Fig. 18.01

Liking
(Intimacy alone)

Romantic love
(Intimacy + Passion)

Infatuation
(Passion alone)

Consummate
love
(Intimacy +
Passion +
Decision/
Commitment)

Fatuous love
(Passion + Decision/
Commitment)

Companionate love
(Intimacy + Decision/
Commitment)

Empty love
(Decision/Commitment
alone)

(Figure adapted from Sternberg, 1988, p. 122)

Westen, 2e Fig. 18.02

© 1999 John Wiley and Sons, Inc.

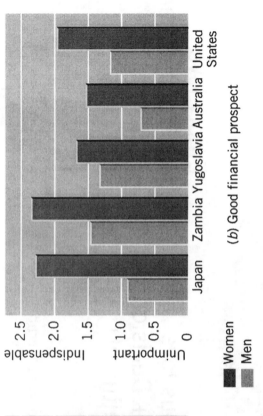

(a) Physical attractiveness

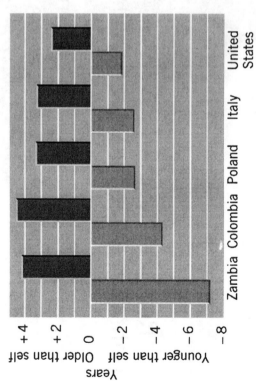

(b) Good financial prospect

(c) Age difference preferred between self and spouse

Women

Men

(Figure adapted from Buss and Schmitt, 1993, pp. 204–232)

Westen, 2e Fig. 18.03

© 1999 John Wiley and Sons, Inc.

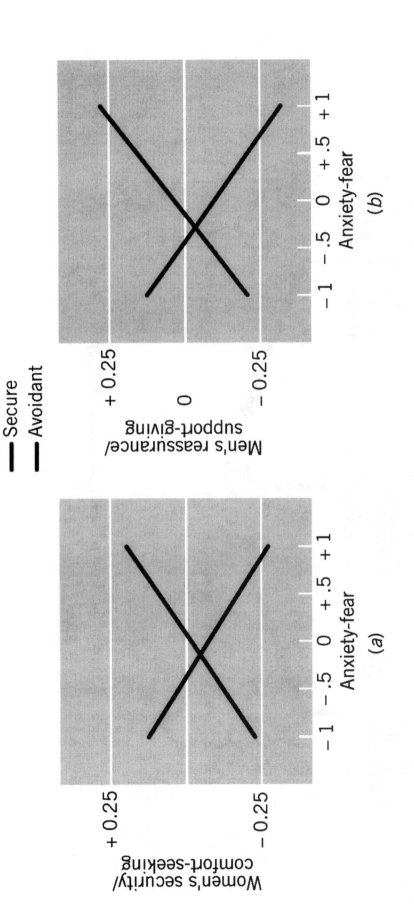

Secure
Avoidant

Women's security/
comfort-seeking

Anxiety-fear
(a)

Men's reassurance/
support-giving

Anxiety-fear
(b)

(Figure adapted from Simpson, et at., 1992, p. 440)

Westen, 2e Fig. 18.04

© 1999 John Wiley and Sons, Inc.

STEP 1
Does the person notice the event?

"Maybe it's nothing."
"It's impolite to stare."

STEP 2
Does the person interpret the situation as an emergency?

"It couldn't be an emergency, or someone would be doing something."
"It could be a hoax."

STEP 3
Does the person take personal responsibility?

"Someone else will call the appropriate authority."
"I don't want to get involved."

Presence of others taking no action

Intervention

No intervention

(Figure adapted from Darley & Latane, 1968, pp. 70-71)

Westen, 2e Fig. 18.05

© 1999 John Wiley and Sons, Inc.

234

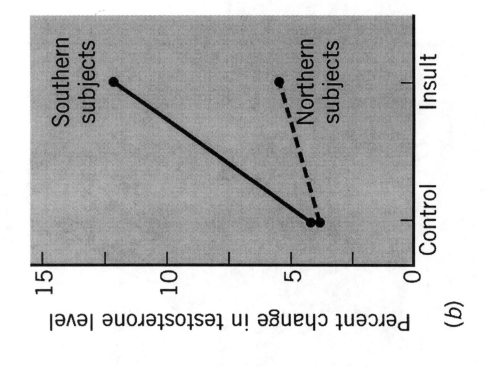

(b)

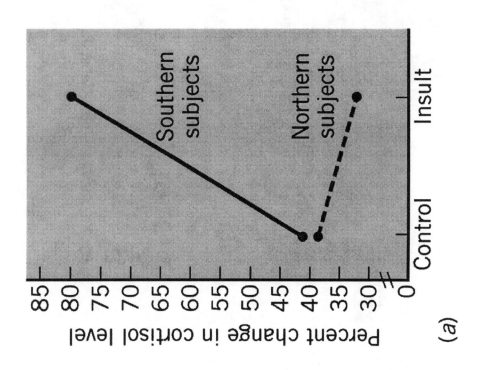

(a)

Westen, 2e Fig. 18.06

© 1999 John Wiley and Sons, Inc.

235

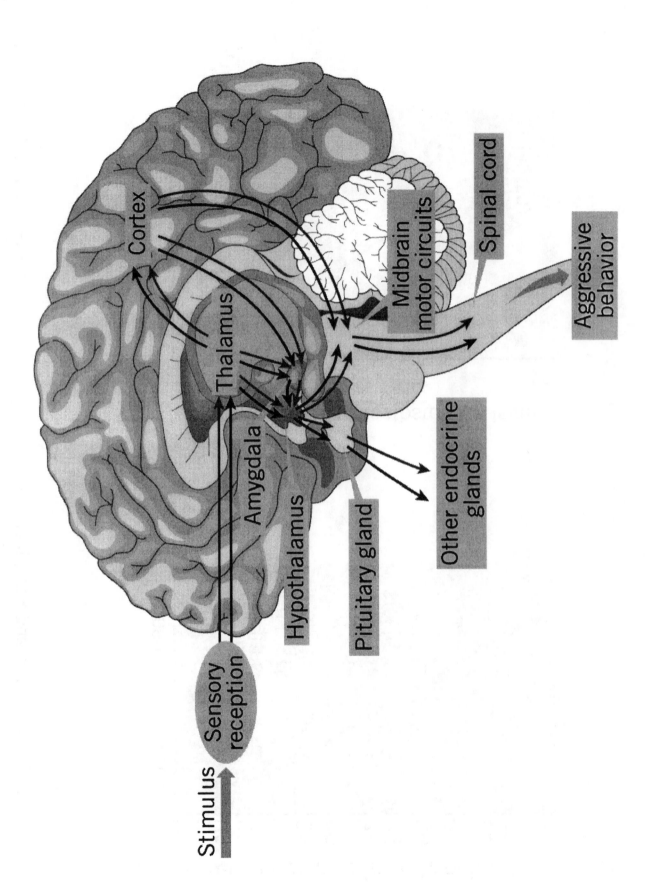

Stimulus → Sensory reception → Cortex / Thalamus / Amygdala / Hypothalamus / Pituitary gland → Midbrain motor circuits / Spinal cord / Other endocrine glands → Aggressive behavior

Westen, 2e Fig. 18.07

© 1999 John Wiley and Sons, Inc.

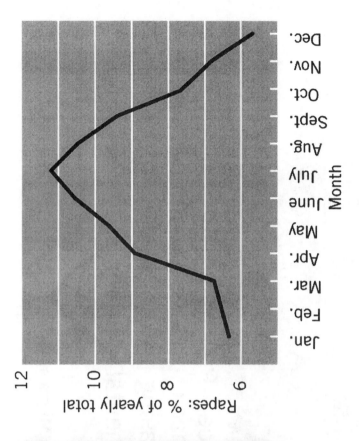

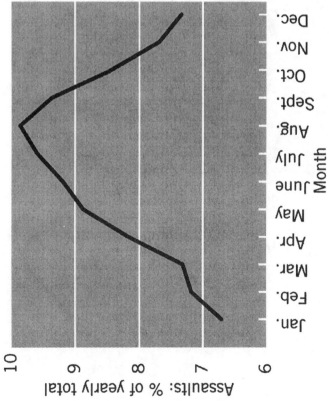

Westen, 2e Fig. 18.08

© 1999 John Wiley and Sons, Inc.

237

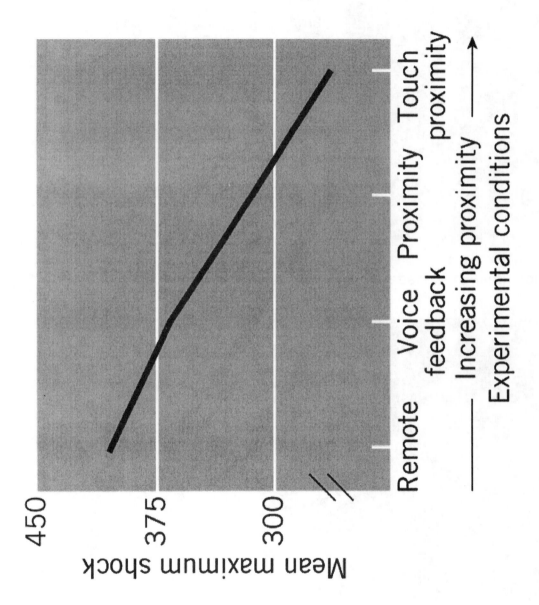

(Figure adapted from Milgram, 1965, pp. 63)

Westen, 2e Fig. 18.09

© 1999 John Wiley and Sons, Inc.

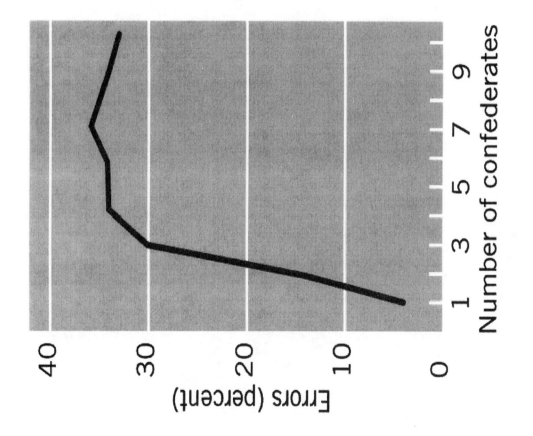

Errors (percent)

Number of confederates

(Figure adapted from Asch, 1955, pp. 193)

Westen, 2e Fig. 18.11

© 1999 John Wiley and Sons, Inc.

✍ Take Note!

✍ Take Note!

✍ Take Note!

✍ Take Note!

✍ Take Note!

✍ Take Note!

✍ Take Note!

✍ Take Note!

✍ Take Note!

✍ Take Note!

✍ Take Note!